Thoughts and Tales That Inspire

Eulene Greenland

World rights reserved. This book or any portion thereof may not be copied or reproduced in any form or manner whatever, except as provided by law, without the written permission of the publisher, except by a reviewer who may quote brief passages in a review.

The author assumes full responsibility for the accuracy of all facts and quotations as cited in this book. The opinions expressed in this book are the author's personal views and interpretations, and do not necessarily reflect those of the publisher.

This book is provided with the understanding that the publisher is not engaged in giving spiritual, legal, medical, or other professional advice. If authoritative advice is needed, the reader should seek the counsel of a competent professional.

Copyright © 2018 Eulene Greenland

Copyright © 2018 TEACH Services, Inc.

ISBN-13: 978-1-4796-0582-8 (Paperback)

ISBN-13: 978-1-4796-0583-5 (ePub)

Library of Congress Control Number: 2016900094

All Scripture is taken from the King James Version Bible. Public domain.

Published by

Contents

Foreword   7

Acknowledgment   9

Childlike Faith   10
And Jesus called a little child unto Him, and set him in the midst of them, And said, Verily I say unto you, Except ye be converted, and become as little children, ye shall not enter into the kingdom of heaven. Whosoever therefore shall humble himself as this little child, the same is greatest in the kingdom of heaven.—Matt. 18:2–4

Daddy's Home!   13
Behold, I stand at the door, and knock: if any man hear My voice, and open the door, I will come in to him, and will sup with him, and he with Me.—Rev. 3:20

Lost at the Mall   15
Yea, though I walk through the valley of the shadow of death, I will fear no evil: for Thou art with me; Thy rod and Thy staff they comfort me.—Ps. 23:4

The Heart House   19
When the unclean spirit is gone out of a man, he walketh through dry places, seeking rest; and finding none, he saith, I will return unto my house whence I came out. And when he cometh, he findeth it swept and garnished. Then goeth he, and taketh to him seven other spirits more wicked than himself; and they enter in, and dwell there: and the last state of that man is worse than the first.—Luke 11:24–26

Planting Season   29
Sow to yourselves in righteousness, reap in mercy; break up your fallow ground: for it is time to seek the LORD, till He come and rain righteousness upon you.—Hosea 10:12

And let us not be weary in well doing: for in due season we shall reap, if we faint not.—Gal. 6:9

Covering the Evidence 34
For God shall bring every work into judgment, with every secret thing, whether it be good or whether it be evil.—Eccl. 12:14

He revealeth the deep and secret things; He knoweth what is in the darkness, and the light dwelleth in Him.—Dan. 2:22

Changing Charlie 39
But I say unto you, Love your enemies, bless them that curse you, do good to them that hate you, and pray for them which despitefully use you, and persecute you; That ye may be the children of your Father which is in heaven: for He maketh His sun to rise on the evil and on the good, and sendeth rain on the just and on the unjust.—Matt. 5:44, 45

Listening to the Holy Spirit 45
"Nevertheless, I tell you the truth; it is expedient for you that I go away: for if I go not away, the Comforter will not come unto you; but if I depart, I will send Him unto you. And when He is come, He will reprove the world of sin, and of righteousness, and of judgment: of sin because they believe not on Me; of righteousness, because I go to My Father, and ye see Me no more; of judgment, because the prince of this world is judged."—John 16:7–11

Sermon: "Remember Lot's Wife" 49
Lot's wife has, over the years, been the object of many jokes and disparaging remarks. However, each Christian needs to examine himself or herself to ensure that we are not at all like Mrs. Lot. "Remember Lot's wife" (Luke 17:32).—Victor Greenland

The Evangelist Dog 54
The beast of the field shall honour Me, the dragons and the owls: because I give waters in the wilderness, and rivers in the desert, to give drink to My people, My chosen.—Isa. 43:20

The Mischievous Guardian Angel 77
There shall no evil befall thee, neither shall any plague come nigh thy dwelling. For He shall give His angels charge over thee, to keep thee in all thy ways. They shall bear thee up in their hands, lest thou dash thy foot against a stone.—Ps. 91:10–12

The Crosses   81
Come unto Me, all ye that labour and are heavy laden, and I will give you rest. Take My yoke upon you, and learn of Me; for I am meek and lowly in heart: and ye shall find rest unto your souls. For My yoke is easy, and My burden is light.—Matt. 11:28–30

The Soursop Tree: Elder Spencer's Testimony   86
He that is faithful in that which is least is faithful also in much: and he that is unjust in the least is unjust also in much.
—Luke 16:10

Forgiveness: Hensler's Change of Heart   91
Judge not, and ye shall not be judged: condemn not, and ye shall not be condemned: forgive, and ye shall be forgiven.—Luke 6:37

The Cobwebs   98
No man, having put his hand to the plough, and looking back, is fit for the kingdom of God.—Luke 9:62

Giving all diligence, add to your faith virtue; and to virtue knowledge; And to knowledge temperance; and to temperance patience; and to patience godliness; And to godliness brotherly kindness; and to brotherly kindness charity. For if these things be in you, and abound, they make you that ye shall neither be barren nor unfruitful in the knowledge of our Lord Jesus Christ.—2 Peter 1:6–8

What Grace Really Means   102
For God so loved the world, that He gave His only begotten Son, that whosoever believeth in Him should not perish, but have everlasting life. For God sent not His Son into the world to condemn the world; but that the world through Him might be saved.—John 3:16, 17

Touched by an Angel: Eulene's Testimony   114
But the Comforter, which is the Holy Ghost, whom the Father will send in My name, He shall teach you all things, and bring all things to your remembrance, whatsoever I have said unto you.—John 14:26

Howbeit when He, the Spirit of truth, is come, He will guide you into all truth: for He shall not speak of Himself; but whatsoever He shall hear, that shall He speak: and He will shew you things to come.— John 16:13

Dedicated to my daughter, Kerrolyn Melanie Antoya Patricia, in thankful acknowledgement of the way the Lord has preserved you, and with the prayer that you will give yourself totally to Him.

Foreword

As we journey in this life toward the Promised Land, we are constantly being buffeted by winds of strife and disappointment, by unforeseen dips and bumps in the road, and by blind corners.

We know we have the Word of God and the presence of the Holy Spirit to guide and comfort us, but sometimes it is a thought or testimony of God's goodness from a fellow believer, shared in the moment or in times past, that comes to mind and cheers us up when we would otherwise be despondent.

Some of the thoughts and tales in this collection have been recounted over a period of half a century. I have had the decided pleasure and privilege of recalling them in moments when cares and challenges would appear to daunt my zeal for life. These experiences have been truly inspiring, reminding me that God shall supply all my needs, according to His riches in glory. They remind me that God will never leave us or forsake us; that Christ has gone to prepare a place for us and that He *is* coming back to receive us unto Himself, so that where He is, we will be also. They also remind us that if we do His commandments, we will have the right to the tree of life and will enter through one of the 12 gates into the city whose builder and maker is God.

Most of the stories are true. The others have true principles. Some stories were told to me firsthand, while some had been told and retold until they reached me, somewhat changed from the way they were originally related. In any event, even the firsthand stories that were told to me may have suffered from lapses in my memory. So, a few details may have been altered; however, the real lessons to be learned remain indelibly etched in my mind, and I hope that they will benefit all those who are in need of a reminder of the great lengths to which our Savior has gone—and will go—to save us.

The poems, for the most part, are original creations of my son, Kerrol Victor Andred St. Aubyn. His main source for inspiration was, and continues to be, the Holy Scriptures.

The sermonette, by my husband, Victor, encourages us to be ever ready for the Lord's coming.

These stories, plus the other thoughts presented, are aimed at the Christian traveler who is having a wonderful time with the Lord but experiencing hate and rejection from the world. May these tales raise your experience to higher ground. May you be given discernment and the courage to say, with the apostle Paul, "I am not ashamed: for I know whom I have believed, and am persuaded that He is able to keep that which I have committed unto Him against that day" (2 Tim. 1:12). They are also aimed at the follower of Christ who finds the way a little rough, the one who has become discouraged about his or her relationship with Christ. After reading the thoughts and tales, may you, along with the apostle Paul, declare, "I am persuaded that neither death, nor life, nor angels, nor principalities, nor powers, nor things present, nor things to come, nor height, nor depth, nor any other creature, shall separate [me] from the love of God, which is in Christ Jesus our Lord" (Rom. 8:38, 39). Then, especially to the one who sees this path as too daunting to even embark on, I want to say, "O taste and see that the Lord is good. Blessed is the man who trusteth in Him" (Ps. 34:8).

In other words, it is my hope that everyone who reads this book will be drawn closer to the Savior.

Acknowledgment

You, no doubt, have heard people who receive various awards say something like, "Thanks, first of all, to God." Well, never before has such a statement been more apt than in this case. I had been writing these thoughts and tales over a period of at least five years and had shelved the project because of a lack of funds to publish it. And even though I attempted to publish it on more than one occasion, the Lord would show me, in each respective case, that it was not the right time. So I want to thank Him profusely for bringing all the right circumstances together for the publication of this book and for the angel in disguise whom He used to do it. To my dear, dear Sister Cheryl John, I want to say may God reward you abundantly above more than you can ever ask or think!

E.P.G.

Childlike Faith

—Retold from an experience related by Pastor Arlington Woodburn while he was at Roosevelt Avenue Seventh-day Adventist Church in Kingston, Jamaica, during the 1980s.

It was Monday evening, about 6:45 p.m. I sighed with relief as I pulled into my driveway. It was summer, and the sun was far from setting. Its warm rays streamed from the windshield of the car and almost blinded me as I gathered my briefcase and documents. I had attended a workers' council at the conference office that day, and there were several matters that I needed to either begin or continue to work on right way.

"No rest for the weary," I groaned.

Gathering my load of books and papers, I tried desperately to assume a sunny disposition in order to greet my wife and two daughters. The girls would want me to check their homework, the younger would certainly want me to read her a story before she went to sleep, and, of course, there would be the tasks my wife had for me to do.

Straightening from the car and using my left foot to push the door shut, I started up toward the front door, a little disappointed that no one seemed to have heard me drive in, since there was not the usual excited "Daddy's home!" and rush to greet me. However, as I started up the walkway to the house, I heard a "Hi, Daddy," coming from somewhere above my head.

It was my younger daughter, six-year-old Anjay. She waved at me from among the branches of the Saint Julian mango tree that grew in our front yard. From this tree we enjoyed countless succulent ripe fruit each year, and among its many branches, the girls had spent many fun-filled hours.

"Hi, honey," I called. I had forgotten that my arms were full, and I almost waved back. "What are you doing up there?" I knew there were no fruits on the tree at that time.

"Waiting for you," was her quick response.

I was both pleased and surprised by the response. Suddenly, looking up into her sweet, innocent face, I forgot the tedious and hectic day I had had, the long list of tasks I still had to complete, and how tired I was.

Without thinking, I grinned at her said, "Jump, and I'll catch you."

Before the words were out of my mouth, I was amazed to see the falling form of my precious child hurtling toward me. For a while, time stood still as my thoughts raced. Anjay was no lightweight, and with the added gravitational boost, I would need to be stopping close to 100 pounds.

How could I have been so stupid? I silently scolded myself that very moment. *What shall I do? Oh, dear God, help me!*

Suddenly, I felt an inexplicable calm come over me. Without realizing it, I let go of the books, papers, and briefcase I had in my hands and reached out to catch my daughter as she literally flew toward me.

"Please, God, let me hold on to her," I prayed. And miraculously, I found the strength, and I didn't fall.

As I gently set my precious daughter to her feet, I looked into her eyes and said, "You jumped! Why did you jump?"

Her trusting eyes met mine, and she gently smiled and said, "You told me to."

That night, after everyone else had gone to bed, I relived the experience.

Faith like that of a child; childlike faith—that's what she had. That's what had caused her to unhesitatingly obey me, and that's what we all need, I mused.

With my adult preconceived notions and learned behaviors, I never would have jumped at such a simple prompting, and I certainly had not expected my daughter to jump.

Anjay had total faith that her dad would catch her. Isn't that the faith we all ought to have in our heavenly Father? We ought to simply take Him at His word, no questions asked. If He says, "Jump!" we shouldn't even have to ask, "How high, Lord?" We should know that He knows that we would jump to the best of our ability.

In Matthew 21, when Jesus, on finding no fruit on the fig, cursed the tree and it dried up, His disciples marveled at this. But Jesus told them, *"Verily I say unto you, If ye have faith and doubt not, ye shall not only do this which is done to the fig tree, but also if ye shall say unto this mountain, Be thou removed, and be thou cast into the sea; it shall be done. And all things, whatsoever ye ask in prayer, believing, ye shall receive"* (verses 21, 22).

Dear Friend, let us ask the Holy Spirit to help us develop childlike faith. Let us trust in the Lord with all our hearts and lean not unto our own understanding. In all our ways, let us acknowledge Him and allow Him to direct our paths (see Prov. 2:5, 6).

"Psalm 1"
In the Holy Bible, it can be read
That he who walks not with the ungodly is blessed,
That a man who finds delight in the Lord
And day and night meditates on His Word,
Shall not fail but shall always prosper.
He shall be like a tree planted by much water.

There is something that I would like to share,
An experience that I treasure and hold dear,
And it is the day I met Jesus,
When I realized that He left heaven just to come to save us.
And since then I've been witnessing
In an attempt to let people know where I've been,
So they can have joy in Christ, too,
And this is an offer from God to me and you.

—K.V.A. St. A. Greenland

Daddy's Home!

—*From an experience related by Kerrol Greenland*

Working as a deliveryman for a large stationery corporation meant my days were always long, and sometimes they could be very trying. Examples of commonplace challenges I dealt with included being given an incorrect address, not being able to find the location, the customer refusing the shipment for various reasons, and a host of others annoyances.

On this particular day, everything that could go wrong did. I had to return to the depot twice to pick up packages that had to be delivered that day or the customer would not accept them. Then, in addition to my regular route, I had to complete the route of a driver who had become ill.

Finally, it was evening, and I was just about to return to the depot when I received a call from base, asking me to rendezvous with another driver and collect a package from him to be delivered early the following morning. I protested but was told that the package was for a really important customer and there was nobody else on whom they could rely. So I went.

I arrived at the meeting spot a full five minutes before the agreed-upon time and waited a full hour without seeing anyone. By then the dispatcher had gone home, and it took several calls for me to finally find out that this driver had decided not to meet me, as he still had other deliveries to make. I really was not pleased to hear that they were asking me to leave earlier than usual the following morning in order to pick up the elusive package.

I was even more disturbed as I drove home. At no time is the traffic on Highway 75, between Miami and Broward County, Florida, easy flowing, but that evening my patience, driving skill, and faith were severely tested. By the time I arrived at my front door, I was fuming and mad at the world.

I fumbled for my door key, inserted it, and turned the lock. Suddenly, from behind the door, I heard a shriek of delight, and as I pushed open the door, my eighteen-month-old son, Ajani, dashed toward me, wrapped his little arms around my legs, and sang, "Daddy's home!"

It was music to my heart. It was a soothing balm to my aching joints and muscles. It was like cooling water over my smoldering temperament and a detangler to my knotted nerves. Suddenly, the day was beautiful.

When mothers of Salem their children brought to Jesus,
The stern disciples drove them back and bade them to depart:
But Jesus saw them ere they fled and sweetly smiled and kindly said,
"Suffer the little children to come unto Me.

"For I will receive them and put them in My bosom;
I'll be a Shepherd to these lambs, O drive them not away.
For if their hearts to Me they give, they shall with Me in glory live;
Suffer the little children to come unto Me."

How kind was our Savior to bid these children welcome!
But there are many thousands who have never heard His name;
The Bible they have never read; they know not that the Savior said,
"Suffer the little children to come unto Me."

O soon may the heathen of every tribe and nation
Fulfill Thy bless-ed Word and cast their idols all away!
O shine upon them from above and show Thyself a God of love,
Teach the little children to come unto Thee!
—*William M. Hutchings, 1850*

Dear Friend, can you imagine the joy unspeakable we'll all experience as our heavenly Father and our Savior will gather us to themselves? At that point we will be able to say that all we have gone through was trivial in comparison to what they have prepared for us. It *will* all be worth it! Let us respond to our Savior now as He knocks at our door. Let us open to Him now so that when He returns to this earth, He can welcome us to His home!

Lost at the Mall

—From an experience related by Pastor Linton Williams

Three-year-old Deedra was like any other preschooler: full of energy, curious about everything, and forever wanting to know "Why?" Her parents loved her dearly and "wouldn't trade her for the world." Deedra was delighted when her dad took her for a ride in his car, and she especially loved when they went to the mall, since she knew that that treat would be topped with an ice cream cone or some cotton candy.

One evening Mom and Dad had to go to the mall, and although Deedra had been very engrossed in playing with her toys, she didn't ask, "But why?" when Mom told her to put her toys away and come to be cleaned up. She saw the car keys in Dad's hands and noticed that Mom had changed her dress. She knew what that meant.

Soon, safely strapped in her seat, Deedra was joyously watching the houses and trees and people and other vehicles zip by.

She tried counting the cars that passed by: "One ... two ... seven ... nine ... ten!"

"There's a blue car, and there's a red car," her mom pointed out, and the car slowed to a halt.

Dad asked, "What does that sign say, Deedra?"

"Stop!" she shouted, then mimicked her dad's voice, "Always stop at the stop sign."

"Or what will happen?" her dad asked.

"You will get a ticket!" she said, sternly wagging her finger at him.

In this manner they soon completed the fifteen-minute journey, and Dad found a space near the entrance of the busy parking lot. Deedra's eyes widened as she watched the shoppers rushing to and fro with their shopping carts and bags. She started bouncing around in her seat.

"Deedra, please stay still," Mom pleaded, as she stepped from the car and went to the open car trunk. In the meantime, Dad got out and went to the backseat.

"Hold still, love, while I unbuckle you," he said as he did just that, even though there was no holding still for Deedra. She was wiggling and straining to get free.

"Wait a minute," Mom said. "Dear, I thought you had put the shopping bags here in the trunk. I don't see them now."

Dad raised his head and leaned over to the back of the car. "I thought I had put them there," he said thoughtfully, but then he remembered. "Oh, I left them on the kitchen table," he said patting his forehead and walking towards his wife.

"Sorry, Hon'," he said meekly. "I don't know what I was thinking. As soon as you gave them to me, I placed them on the table and promptly forgot about them."

"Well, we'll just have to buy some more," she said in resignation. "Come on. Get Deedra and let's go."

Dad bent his head and looked into the car to complete the unbuckling of his daughter's car seat, then straightened with a puzzled look on his face.

"Where's Deedra?" he asked his wife.

"Isn't she in the car? You were just unbuckling her," said his wife, her voice and face showing her alarm.

They both began running around their car and then around other cars in the lot, shouting their daughter's name. Passersby looked at them strangely, wondering what was happening.

"Please, sir, ... ma'am, have you seen a little girl wandering by herself? She is about this high," Dad said, indicating her height. "And she's wearing a pink jumpsuit with pink ribbons in her hair," he finished lamely.

His wife was doing the same thing on the other side of the parking lot, and she was in tears.

No one had seen the little girl. How could she have disappeared so quickly? What had become of her? They had only taken their eyes off her for one minute at most.

After what seemed like a lifetime but in reality was only ten minutes, Deedra's parents stopped rushing around and tried to decide what to do. They knew they had to get help, but they did not want to leave the lot. Out of sheer exhaustion, they both sat down on a concrete embankment near their car.

"Let us pray," Dad said gently. They both knelt there on the ground and with tightly clasped hands, prayed silently, too overcome to put their thoughts into audible words.

"Mom, Dad—I was looking for you!"

Their eyes flew open as they both heard the voice of their beloved child. There she was, standing beside a tall gentleman who held on to her with his left hand while holding a rather heavy-looking shopping bag in his right hand.

"Deedra!" they both shouted, then got up and rushed to scoop her up in both their arms. They cried and hugged and cried and hugged some more while the stranger stood, waiting with thinly veiled irritation.

"Ahem," he cleared his throat. "I have to go."

"Please, sir, ... how ... where ...? They didn't know what to ask.

The man seemed very impatient. "I have to be at work soon," he said. "I stopped at the supermarket to pick up these items," he said, motioning toward his bag. "As soon as I rounded that corner," he pointed with his free hand, "I heard a little voice saying 'Daddy, wait for me.' I looked behind me and saw this little girl running hard to catch up with me. I didn't know what to do. I thought of leaving her with the first police patrol car I saw, but I finally decided—something told me to return here," he said, obviously glad that his forced wardenship was over.

"Please, sir, we don't know how to thank you," both parents gushed. "What can we do?" they asked.

"Take better care of you child in the future," he said sternly and strode off.

Deedra's parents stared at his disappearing back, speechless. Suddenly it all made sense to Dad. The man rapidly walking away was roughly his height. They were both wearing similar-looking blue jeans and white loafers, and also, the man's gait was not unlike his own. The little girl had apparently freed herself from the seat while he was speaking to his wife. She had slidden from the car, and then, seeing the stranger passing by the car at that moment and not being able to see clearly above the man's waist, she had followed him, mistakenly thinking he was her dad.

Again they knelt, and this time they sent up a prayer of gratitude to God that they had lost their daughter and found her again unharmed! They both resolved to never again take their eyes off their precious child.

Dear Friend, our heavenly Father is always there to guide and protect us. He keeps us in the palm of His hand and sends His angels to guide our every step. Even when things go horribly wrong, we can be assured that but for His intervention, it would be far worse. What a wonderful God we serve!

> He's got the whole world in His hands;
> He's got you and me, Brother, in His hands;
> He's got you and me, Sister, in His hands;
> He's go the tiny, tiny baby in His hands;
> He's got the whole world in His hands.

The Heart House

Christ must have complete control and rulership over our heart house, or the devil will take it over.

Ken had attended every night of the summer evangelistic meetings held at his church. He had listened attentively to the speaker each night and had felt convicted about his sinful life—not that a nine-year-old boy had had much time to commit a great deal of sins—but he had told more than his "fair share" of lies to his parents, especially when his mom would ask, "Did you wash your hands?" He had done more than a negligible amount of coveting, especially when his friend John got a new version of the latest toy, seemingly every week, since John's parents were wealthy and were always travelling all over the world. Ken had committed a great deal of bearing false witness against his neighbor—at least against his big brother, Tim, when Tim wanted to go and play with his friends and didn't want his little brother tagging along.

"Go back!" Tim would say. "The boys are going to be rough when they play, and you're going to tell Mom that they hit you, and she's going to tell me no the next time I ask her to let me go out and play."

Ken would run back to the house bawling his eyes out. Mom would come running, wanting to know, "What's wrong?"

Ken would spin a tale of how Tim had wrung his arm and pushed him to the ground, and by then his arm would have a red streak, and perhaps he would even skin his knee against the rough cement pavement to make his story more convincing.

Mom would get upset and mete out some punishment to Tim, who had learned a long time ago that he couldn't defend himself against the "evidence," but he would chalk up another item for which he would get even with his little brother when his parents weren't around.

Ken was also a little concerned about his observance of the first commandment,[1] especially when he thought of his new Sony PlayStation. Even

---

1 "I am the Lord thy God, ... Thou shalt have no other gods before me" (Exod. 20:2, 3).

though he had received it as a gift several months ago, he still kept in its original packaging. It was still shiny and new, mainly because he didn't play with it much and he certainly allowed no one else to touch it. He simply liked to look at it and polish the controls. In fact, many evenings when his parents thought he was in his room studying his memory verse for the week, Ken simply sat and admired his new toy.

With respect to the Sabbath, the words "Remember the Sabbath day to keep it holy" echoed in his mind as he remembered the many Sabbath afternoons when, at Junior AY,[2] he had sat with some of his friends at the back of the room and done his best to disrupt the afternoon's program, deriving great pleasure from the frustrated outbursts of the Junior AY leader.

So Ken had indeed led a checkered life. He fully realized that he needed to ask Jesus to forgive him for his sins. He remembered the words of the song that was sung at the conclusion of the meeting each night:

"Let Jesus Come Into Your Heart"
If you are tired of the load of your sin,
Let Jesus come into your heart;
If you desire a new life to begin,
Let Jesus come into your heart.

[Refrain]
Just now, your doubtings give o'er;
Just now, reject Him no more;
Just now, throw open the door;
Let Jesus come into your heart.

If it's for purity now that you sigh,
Let Jesus come into your heart;
Fountains for cleansing are flowing nearby,
Let Jesus come into your heart.

[Refrain]
If there's a tempest your voice cannot still,
Let Jesus come into your heart;

---

[2] AY refers to Adventist Youth, which are youth group meetings commonly held at Seventh-day Adventist churches on Saturday (Sabbath) afternoons.

If there's a void this world never can fill,
Let Jesus come into your heart.

[Refrain]
If you would join the glad songs of the blest,
Let Jesus come into your heart;
If you would enter the mansions of rest,
Let Jesus come into your heart.

[Refrain]

—*Leila N. Morris, 1898*

To let Jesus come into his heart was something that he desperately wanted to do. That night, as his dad came to say goodnight, Ken asked, "Dad, do you think I'm a sinner?"

"Well, Son, the Bible says that all have sinned, so we are all sinners. You are a sinner, and I'm a sinner," his dad said.

"You're a sinner?" Ken's eyes widened "I've never seen you do anything wrong!"

Oh, I've done my fair share of sinning," his dad smiled, "especially when I was about your age. But I have asked Jesus to forgive me of all my sins and to come and take charge of my heart house and live there," he said.

"I would love to have Jesus living in my heart," Ken said, wistfully.

"Well, let's ask Him right now," his dad said.

Together, father and son knelt by Ken's bedside and the little boy prayed, "Dear Jesus, I am so sorry for all the wrong things I've done. Please forgive me for all my sins and come and live in my heart, dear Lord. I promise I will keep it very clean for You. Thank You, Lord. Amen."

His father prayed, "Heavenly Father, you've heard the prayer of my dear son. I ask that you grant him his petition, Lord, and help him to be a true representative of you from now on. In Jesus' name I pray. Amen."

Dad stayed a few minutes more talking with his son, and as he turned to leave the room, he said, "Remember now, Ken, Jesus does not want to be a guest in your heart. He wants to be the owner."

Ken drifted off to sleep with those words ringing in his ears.

Then he heard a gentle knock at his door. He tiptoed over and opened the door and peered out into the darkened hall. It was Jesus! The Savior's loving gaze seemed to go right through him.

"Hello, Ken. I am here to enter your heart house. Are your ready for Me?"

"Oh yes, Lord Jesus. Come right in!" Ken said delightedly. He stepped back and opened the door wider. Jesus entered and stood looking at him expectantly.

"Please sit down," Ken said, sweeping some toys off a chair.

"Is this where you want Me to stay?" Jesus asked.

W-e-ll, yes. Make yourself comfortable right there," Ken said, a little unsure of himself.

Jesus settled down in the chair and started looking around. At once, Ken felt self- conscious and started picking up stray toys and clothes.

"Things are a little bit untidy right now, but I'll soon fix them," he told the Savior. As he moved around the room, he came to a box that was sitting on the most comfortable chair in the room. For a moment he forgot about Jesus as he lovingly removed the contents of the box and began to wipe the already shiny gadget.

Thou shalt have no other gods before Me. Jesus did not say the words, but Ken looked straight at Him as they came to his mind.

"Lord Jesus," he said tentatively, "I have not given You the place You deserve. I have been treating this PlayStation like a god. Please forgive me. With that, he replaced the toy in the box and placed the box on the shelf with all his other toys. He dusted the chair and invited the Savior to sit there. Then he continued straightening his room.

Suddenly, there was a loud knock at the front door. Ken forgot what he was doing and dashed out of the room. He saw his brother, Tim, opening the front door.

"Hi, Tim," said Jeffrey.

"Hi, Tim," said Sid. Both boys were Tim's best friends.

"Hi, guys. What's up?" said Tim.

"We're going over to the park to pitch ball," said John. "Do you want to come along?"

"Of course! I'll go and ask Mom," Tim said as his face brightened.

"I'm coming, too," Ken called as he bounded down the stairs.

"Oh no, you're not!" Tim said. Go play with your own friends."

Ken let out a scream as he prepared to put on a performance for his mom.

Thou shalt not bear false witness against thy neighbor, Ken remembered. He looked up to see Jesus looking down at him through his open bedroom door. He also remembered his father's words: *"Ken, Jesus doesn't want to be a guest in your house. He wants to be the owner."*

"Lord, perhaps you will be more comfortable in the living room," he said. "Please come and sit in this chair."

The Lord obligingly came downstairs and sat in the chair Ken pointed to. In the meantime, Tim and his friends went off to the park. Luckily, his mom had been in the basement and had not heard the commotion, so Ken didn't have to lie. He felt relieved.

As he stood there wondering what to do next, the doorbell rang again. This time it was his friend John, wanting to show off his latest new toy. It was a battery-operated helicopter with a remote control that sent it soaring high above their heads. Ken felt resentment well up in him as John rambled on and on about the things the mechanical toy could do.

"I don't want to hear anything about your silly chopper," he told a surprised John, as Ken pushed the toy back toward him.

Thou shalt not covet ... any thing that is thy neighbor's.[3]

Again Ken first sensed and then saw that the Savior was looking at him. "I'm sorry I said that," he told his friend. I'm not in the mood to play with your toy right now; perhaps later. Let's go outside and play ball."

A relieved John readily agreed, and the two filed outside. They were soon playing a fast-paced game of catch. As Ken reached for a ball that had been vigorously hurled at him, he took his eyes off the ball for a brief moment, and the ball plummeted into his chest.

"Ow! Are you trying to kill me?" he cried. He strode over to John and shoved him.

"It's your fault! You took your eyes off the ball!" John exclaimed, shoving him back.

"But you threw it too hard!" Ken retorted, shoving him again.

"Well, your throw was hard, too!" John replied, shoving his friend once more.

Soon both boys were engaged in a tussle and rolling around on the ground.

Thou shalt love thy neighbor as thyself.[4]

Something told Ken to look toward the house. There was Jesus looking disapprovingly at them through an open window. He quickly let go of John's flailing arms. As he did so, John's right fist caught Ken flush in his left eye as the younger boy struggled to free himself. Ken clutched at his face, and, finally free, John dashed toward the house.

---

3 Exod. 20:17.
4 Matt. 22:39; cf. Lev. 19:18.

"Lord, could You come out here a minute, please?" Ken asked.

The Savior willingly came at his bidding.

"Could You please sit on this mound? I think if you're here, John will play fair," he said.

"Are you sure you have been playing fair?" the Savior asked.

Ken considered for a minute, then simply said, "I'm sorry; I shoved him first."

"You need to tell that to John," the Savior said.

"I'll tell him when he comes back outside," Ken said, but at that moment, his mom called him inside. He ran to her, already composing an explanation as to why he had been fighting with his friend.

Surprisingly, his mom did not ask him anything about the fight. She merely said, "Go and wash your hands while I fix you something to eat."

As he walked past the kitchen, Ken was surprised to see John seated at the kitchen table, enjoying a generous helping of ice cream. Ken didn't have to look twice to see that it was his favorite flavor, pecan-almond. He increased his pace to the bathroom, and although he was tempted to lie to his mom about washing his hands, he thought of the treat awaiting him and of the Savior waiting outside, and he gave himself a good scrub, then eagerly went to the kitchen.

Ken found John finishing his ice cream with a contented look on his face. His face was far from contented, however, when he discovered that his treat was a mere peanut butter sandwich.

"Where's my ice cream?" he asked his mom

"You will have some later. Eat your sandwich now," his mom said.

"But that's not fair! You're not being fair! You gave him all that ice cream, and you couldn't give me some!" he wailed and sent looks of resentment toward his mom. He would have said much more, but suddenly he felt compelled to look outside.

Jesus was still sitting on the mound where he had left Him, but Ken could hear the Savior saying to him, "Honor thy father and thy mother…"

"I'm sorry, Mom. Please forgive me," he quickly said, before his mother could compose a response to his outburst, adding, "Can I go outside to eat my sandwich?"

"I was about to send you to your room *without* your sandwich. But, OK, you may go outside," his mom said.

Ken quickly went to Jesus. "Lord, why am I still misbehaving, even though I have asked You to come and live with me?" he asked.

The Heart House

"Do you remember what your father said as he told you goodnight?" Jesus asked, adding, "He told you that you cannot have Me as just a guest in your heart house. If you treat Me as only a guest, there is nothing I can do about the bad things you continue to do."

"What should I do, then?" Ken asked, perplexed.

"You have to turn control over to Me," Jesus said. You may put Me to sit in your best chair in the best room. But unless you give Me total control of your entire heart house, there is nothing I can do when the bad habits take over."

"Lord, I do not want to continue misbehaving. I really want You to be in charge," Ken said earnestly. "What shall I do?"

"Just give Me permission to move freely up and down and around your heart house," the Savior said.

"You have it. I am giving you total control now," Ken said. The Savior smiled and stretched out His hand. Ken put his hand in the Master's, and together they walked back to the house. John was now playing with his new toy.

"Wow! That sure is so cool!" said Ken and was surprised that he did not feel jealous anymore.

"Would you like to play with it?" John asked.

"Sure!" Ken said, and together the two boys sat in the sofa. Both boys took turns controlling the mechanical toy, with Jesus looking over their shoulders.

"John, I'm sorry I was mean to you. Can you forgive me?" Ken finally said as he gave his friend a disarming smile.

John was taken aback but smiled. "Of course I forgive you. You're my best friend," he said.

Soon Mom came into the room. She had her arms full of freshly laundered clothes. Ken jumped to his feet.

"Let me help you, Mom," he said, as he reached up and relieved his mother of her load. "I'll fold them and put them away for you," he offered.

"Well! I never… What never happens in a year happens in a day. Since when have you become so helpful?" his mother asked, beaming at him.

"Since I gave Jesus full control of my heart house," Ken said. "From now on, He's going to help me to be really helpful and obedient to you," he promised.

"Praise the Lord! You have made me so happy, Son," Ken's mother said as she hugged him.

As Ken busied himself with the laundry, there was a loud commotion outside as Tim burst through the door. He was sweaty and rather scruffy looking from his romp in the park.

"Hi, Tim, did you have a good time?" Ken asked.

"What's it to you?" Tim asked warily. He was not used to friendliness from his little brother.

"Oh, I just hope that you enjoyed your game," Ken said. "And I'm really sorry I was so mean this morning. Please forgive me," he smiled disarmingly at his big brother.

"Wait a minute. What's happening here?" Tim sounded confused.

"Well, it's like this: I asked Jesus to take control of my heart, and from now on He is going to help me to be really, really nice to you," Ken said sweetly.

"That's the best news I've heard in a long time," Tim said. He smiled and patted his brother on his back. "Things are going to be a whole lot better around here," he said with relief.

Ken looked at Jesus, and the Savior was smiling, too.

"Lord Jesus, from now on I'm giving You full control of my heart house. Please have Your own way and help me to do the right thing at all times," the little boy said.

"I will never leave you nor forsake you. I will be with you always," the Savior said as He brushed His palm across Ken's face.

"Thank you, Lord," Ken said, and he smiled broadly as he felt the warmth of the Savior's touch on his face.

As the heat on his face intensified, Ken opened his eyes to see that the light of the sun was streaming through his window.

"Ken, are you awake, Son? It's time to get up." His dad knocked gently on the door and called out to his son.

The lad sprang from his bed and ran to his dad.

"Dad, I had the most wonderful dream. I dreamed that I gave Jesus full control of my heart house. From now on He is the owner and ruler of my heart house, and He says He will always be with me and will help me to do the right thing!" he exclaimed

"Let's thank Him for that. Let's pray together."

Father and son knelt and prayed to *their* heavenly Father.

Dear Friend, the Savior is waiting to enter our hearts and to be the ruler of our lives. Because He created us with the power of choice, He will not force His will on us; but He will, with alacrity, accept our invitation to enter and establish His presence in our hearts. Won't you say yes to Jesus today? It's a decision that will be life changing now and richly rewarding in the hereafter.

> Dear Lord and Father of mankind,
> Forgive our foolish ways!
> Re-clothe us in our rightful mind,
> In purer lives Thy service find,
> In deeper reverence, praise.
>
> In simple trust like theirs who heard
> Beside the Syrian sea
> The gracious calling of the Lord,
> Let us, like them, without a word
> Rise up and follow Thee.
>
> O Sabbath rest by Galilee!
> O calm of hills above,
> Where Jesus knelt to share with Thee
> The silence of eternity
> Interpreted by love!
>
> With that deep hush subduing all
> Our words and works that drown
> The tender whisper of Thy call,
> As noiseless let Thy blessing fall
> As fell Thy manna down.
>
> Drop Thy still dews of quietness,
> Till all our strivings cease;
> Take from our souls the strain and stress,
> And let our ordered lives confess
> The beauty of Thy peace.
>
> Breathe through the heat of our desire
> Thy coolness and Thy balm;
> Let sense be dumb, let flesh retire;
> Speak through the earthquake, wind, and fire,
> O still, small voice of calm.
>
> *—John Greenleaf Whittier (1807–1892)*

Salvation
Satisfaction comes with salvation;
So do happiness, joy, and peace.
Forget about sinful instances
And, for once, set your mind at ease.

About salvation, there is much to say,
A number of facts that can't be said in one day.
But the most important thing to remember
Is that salvation is not possible without the Savior.

Salvation can be described as a wonderful thing,
A wonderful thing that makes Christians sing.
You can experience this salvation,
But first you must accept Christ's crucifixion

—*K.V.A. St. A. Greenland*

Planting Season

The sun shone warmly through the trees, and a gentle wind tugged at the leaves, making a rustling sound as it cooled the faces of the two children who were bent over in the wide field. Twelve-year-old Jeremy and his ten-year-old sister, Jennifer, were trying their best to complete their chores. They knew they dared not stop, as Aunt Iris would be coming to inspect their handiwork, and she would not be pleased if they were not finished.

It wasn't that Aunt Iris was a hard taskmaster—the opposite, in fact. For three weeks, she had been urging Jerry and Jenny to plant a small portion of their farm with melons and peas. First she had asked them to prepare the plot by using the tiller to turn over the soil. As time went by and they kept breaking their promise to till the ground, Aunt Iris had to do it herself. She had also planted the other crops such as corn, okra, and tomatoes; and she could have planted the melons and the peas, but she wanted her two wards to learn to be responsible and to experience the joy of actually eating crops they had planted.

Jeremy and Jennifer were orphans. Their parents had died tragically in a motor vehicle accident when Jennifer was six years old. Aunt Iris and her husband, Toby, had taken them in and provided them with a lovely home, but within only two years, Uncle Toby suffered a massive heart attack and died. After his death, things became a little difficult for Aunt Iris, but she was determined to keep her niece and nephew. Since money was scarce, she asked them to help her with some of the tasks around the farm.

The trouble was Jeremy and Jennifer were not fond of hard work. They loved their aunt and appreciated all that she did for them, but they really hated doing the chores and tried to avoid doing them whenever they could. As winter turned to spring, the two children loved nothing better than fishing in the small lake on the farm, riding their dirt bikes through the hills behind the farm, and playing on the swing behind the farmhouse. Every opportunity they got, that was what they would do. They would promptly forget whatever they had promised to do and spend their time having fun.

Aunt Iris tried to instill discipline in them by cutting their recreation time, but they simply played through whatever task they were given. "Children," she would plead, "please be more responsible. You simply must help me to do some of the chores. I cannot afford to pay someone to do things that you can do."

They knew she spoke the truth, and they would feel sorry and promise to do better, but the resolve would not last long. This would go on until Aunt Iris really had to put her foot down and insist that unless they followed her instructions, there would be dire consequences. Such was the case that morning. Both had risen from the breakfast table intent on grabbing their dirt bikes and heading for the hills.

"Jeremy and Jennifer, you simply must plant those peas and melons today. We have lost so much time already. If you don't plant them today, they will not have enough time to bear," Aunt Iris said quietly.

There were a few signs to warn them that she was serious. For one, she spoke slowly and quietly. Since she had lost 10 percent of her hearing when a rifle was discharged too close to her head, and especially since she constantly had to be calling out to Jeremy and Jennifer, Aunt Iris was known to speak a little too loudly. Also, she was a fast talker, except when she wanted every word she said to be clearly understood. Finally, she had called them "Jeremy and Jennifer." Normally, she called them "Jerry and Jenny," and when she was in a really good mood, she would say, "Jer and Jen." Whenever she said Jeremy and Jennifer, quietly and slowly, they knew they were skating on thin ice. There was to be no discussion. They were simply to do what she said.

"Yes, ma'am," they both said sheepishly.

Jeremy went to the shed; took two buckets, one with peas, the other with melon seeds; and handed one to his sister. He also took the digging pole, and together they trudged toward the field.

"This is really hateful stuff," Jeremy complained. He was digging the holes, and Jennifer was walking behind him, throwing three or four seeds in each hole. They would do one row on the right and then one on the left.

"The peas on the right and the melons on the left," Aunt Iris had said. "And they had better be done properly. I'll be coming to inspect them when you're done," she had added.

Up and down one row, and down and up another they went, so many times that they soon lost count.

"Man, it seems that the more we sow, the more seeds there are in these buckets," Jennifer said. "I'm tired," she added.

"I'm tired, too," Jeremy said, "but what can we do? Aunt Iris will not be pleased if we do not finish the planting today. Tell you what: Try doubling up on the seeds. Instead of putting three or four seeds, try putting six or eight."

They did just that for a few more rows, but still the seeds in the buckets seemed more than before. Jennifer got so frustrated that she stopped being careful about which seeds went where. Soon melons were going where peas ought to have gone, and peas were going where melons ought to have gone. Then she was scooping up handfuls of seeds and depositing them in the holes.

In this manner they finally emptied the buckets. With great relief they sped back to the house, and without saying anything to Aunt Iris, they quietly took their bikes and pushed them away from the house, only starting the motors when they were some distance away.

Aunt Iris had just finished her cleaning when she heard the motor bikes. Fearing that the children had abandoned their tasks, she walked down to the field and was quite pleased to see the several rows of freshly dug soil. She was so pleased that she decided to prepare a special treat for them. Therefore, they were surprised and delighted when they straggled in much, much later without Aunt Iris scolding them upon arrival. Instead, after she had made them wash up for supper, she ushered them to the table boasting the most delicious dish of chicken and dumplings they had ever tasted. In response to their puzzled looks, Aunt Iris explained how she had doubted that they would plant all the rows of peas and melons. She said to make amends for doubting them, she had made them their favorite dish. What she did not tell them was that to purchase the chicken, she had used funds that she had been saving to purchase a much-needed pair of shoes for herself. And although the children felt a little guilty, they did not tell her that they had done a really terrible job, especially toward the end.

Within a few days, especially after two good downpours, the seeds began to sprout. At first, the two children were thrilled to see the little plants peeping out of the ground, but as time passed, the sloppy job they had done became apparent. Except for the first few rows, peas and melons were popping up everywhere. In some spots so many plants came up that they were unable to thrive.

Aunt Iris was livid. She marched the children down to the garden patch and stood there while they transplanted all the improperly sown seedlings. They hated every minute of it. But afterward, Aunt Iris sat them down and explained how their thoughtless actions had already been costly and how they needed to change.

Jeremy and Jennifer wept as they realized how much their carelessness had hurt their aunt. They told her they did not want to continue being selfish. Aunt Iris told them that she could not help them and neither could they help themselves. But, she said, she knew Someone who could. They eagerly asked if they could meet that person.

This was Aunt Iris's opportunity to tell her wards about her Savior, of how He had taken full control of her life, of how she did only things that pleased Him. It took a long time and many, many questions and answers, but gradually the children came to understand the love of their Savior and His will for them.

WWJD? What Would Jesus Do? Aunt Iris taught Jerry and Jenny to ask themselves this question every time they were faced with a decision. She told them that Jesus would always do the right thing, and so should they. She reminded them that she would not be able to observe and guide their every action, but God would. She taught them the words of this song:

> God is always near me,
> Hearing what I say;
> Knowing all my thoughts and deeds,
> All my work and play.
>
> God is always near me,
> In the darkest night,
> He can see me just the same
> As by midday light.
>
> God is always near me,
> Though so young and small;
> Not a look, or word, or thought,
> But God knows it all.

—*Philip Bliss, 1871*

Finally, the two children learned to rely on the Lord to guide them, and they soon found that His grace was sufficient for them. In fact, it was all they needed. Aunt Iris never again needed to tell them more than once to do anything. In fact, often they would not wait for their guardian to tell them what to do. They would arise early in the morning, set on doing their tasks. And do you know what? They found that after completing their chores, they still had ample time to do all the fun stuff.

Dear Friend, our loving Savior came to this earth and lived a life of example for us; then He said, "Follow Me." He died the death that we should die, so that we can have His eternal life. He says, "Greater love hath no man than this, that a Man laid down His life for His friends. Ye are My friends if ye do whatsoever I command you" (John 15: 13, 14). He also says, "My yoke is easy, and My burden is light" (Matt. 11:30). There is nothing that He requires us to do that He did not do Himself when He walked this earth or that He will not provide us with the resources to accomplish. Let us surrender our will to Him so He can work out His will through us.

Responsibility
There were four friends living together;
They were Everybody, Somebody, Anybody, and Nobody.
There was an important job to be done.
Everybody thought that Someone should do it.
Anyone could have done it, but Nobody did it.
It turned out that there was a real disaster
When Everyone knew about the job to be done;
Anybody could have done it; Somebody should have done it;
But Nobody did it.

—adapted from shorter versions of Charles Osgood's
"A Poem About Responsibility"

Covering the Evidence

Peter stumbled into the kitchen and heaved the heavy baskets he was carrying onto the counter. He had visited the local farmers' market with his mom, and they had purchased several pounds of fresh fruits, nuts, and vegetables. "There are almonds, avocados, apples, bananas, beans, cashews, carrots, and lots of 'wholesome healthy foods'," his mom would say.

Peter was fond enough of all these nuts, fruits, and vegetables, but the one fruit he was absolutely crazy about was the honeydew. They had seen several honeydews being sold at the farmers' market, and he had wanted his mom to purchase them all; but of course, she wouldn't.

"I'm only going to buy one honeydew," his mom had said. "There are so many other things I need to buy. In any event, you are the one who loves honeydews the most, so you'll be the one eating most of this one anyway," she added.

Peter had to admit that that was true, but he still felt that his mom should have gotten two honeydews. *This one's gonna be finished long before the weekend is over*, he thought.

After they had unloaded the groceries, Peter and his sister, Hannah, washed the fruits and vegetables and put them away. He lingered long over the honeydew as he imagined sinking his teeth into its succulent pulp. He couldn't wait!

After supper that evening, Hannah reminded Mom that they should be taking a basket of groceries over to the Joneses. The Joneses were a family who lived on the edge of town. The father had been hit by a truck and had become a paraplegic. The mother had become the sole breadwinner for a family of seven, and they were having a hard time making ends meet. The members of Peter and Hannah's church had voted that each family would take a basket of groceries to the Joneses each week, and it was now the Townsends'—Peter's family's—turn. The problem was, Mrs. Townsend had forgotten about this and had committed to attending a series of meetings at the city council.

"I'm really sorry that I forgot," she said. "That means I'm going to have to ask you to take the basket for me, Peter," she told her son, adding, "Dad will be working late all of this week, and Hannah will be accompanying me to the meetings."

Peter didn't mind going over to the Joneses. They had a boy, Josh, who was nearly his age, and he knew they could enjoy a game of catch before he returned home.

Shortly thereafter, Mrs. Townsend left for her meeting, but not before going through her pantry and filling a large basket with most of the items a family of seven would need for a week.

"Please check to make sure I have everything from this list," she instructed her son, "and if there is anything that you think I've left out, you may put it in. Just text me and let me know first," she added.

After his mom and sister left, Peter watched some television, then he played a video game, and then he listened to some music. He was about to fall asleep, when the phone rang. It was his mom.

"Peter, are you still at home? I thought you would have left by now," she said.

"I ... I'll be leaving in a little while," he said quickly. "As soon as I finish checking these items, I'll leave."

"Have you found anything that I left out?" his mom asked.

Well, ... I was just thinking that if you had bought two honeydews, we could have given them one," he said. He had been thinking of no such thing.

His mother thought for a moment. "Well, tell you what," she said. "Cut the honey dew in half and give the Joneses one half," she said.

Peter's heart sank. That meant there would be even less honeydew for him. But he forced himself to say, "OK, I'll do that."

After he hung up, Peter went for the honeydew and laid it on the kitchen table. He pulled a knife from its block and expertly sliced the fruit in half. Then he scrutinized the two pieces very carefully to see if one side was bigger than the other. They were fairly even, but he carefully wrapped the portion he thought was smaller in cellophane and placed it in the basket. Then he looked at the other half.

"I guess I should taste it to make sure it's fit to be given to anybody," he said to himself, and he did just that. The fact was, though, the slice he took was more than adequate for a mere taste. Well, as was to be expected, the honeydew was good; really, really good. In fact, it was so good that Peter thought he should have another taste.

I'll just have mine now, and the others can take the rest, he thought. So he did. In fact, reasoning to himself that his family did not like honeydews anyway, and in any event, his mom was to blame for buying only one honeydew, Peter sat and consumed the entire half of the honeydew. After that delightful experience, the lad sat and savored the moment before reality intruded.

What would he tell his mom when she asked him about the family's half of the honeydew?

"I'm gonna say I gave the Joneses the whole honeydew," he told himself. He looked around the kitchen: honeydew peel and seeds were all over the counter.

What could he do with the evidence? He got busy and wiped the counter. Then he collected the seeds and peel, wrapped them in paper towels, and took them outside. He was afraid to place them in the garbage bin, as he felt his mother could discover them. Perhaps it was his guilty conscience that caused him to not think straight, or it may have been his realization that it was getting late and his dad would soon be home. Whatever it was, Peter concluded that the best way to cover his crime was to cover the evidence, literally. He quickly ran to the shed, grabbed a small shovel, then went behind the shed and dug a shallow hole, deposited the seeds and the peel therein, and covered the hole, making certain that the ground did not appear as if it had been freshly dug.

He then grabbed the basket and raced from the house, hoping that he would not encounter his dad. He did not and later felt quite good about his cleverness. He declined Josh's challenge to play catch and hurried back home.

As soon as he arrived, he texted his mother: "Gss wht, I didn't want 2 give the Joneses half honeydew so I gave them 1. They say mny thanx for all."

Mrs. Townsend was very surprised but quite pleased by her son's gesture and told him so when she returned from her meeting.

"I promise you," she said to him, "I'll make sure to buy a honeydew especially for you when I go back to the farmers' market."

Peter's conscience bothered him somewhat, but he was too thrilled dwelling on enjoying his very own honeydew to think about what he had done. And he had his honeydew the following week, and he had several honeydews after that. With some difficulty at first, but later with little effort, he managed to quell his guilty conscience.

Eventually, Peter forgot about that afternoon when he had eaten the honeydew and had lied to his mother. But did he get away with it? Let's see. Numbers 32:23 says, in part, "Be sure your sin will find you out."

Mrs. Townsend was out in the yard several weeks later. Fall was coming to a close, and she was making sure to put away some of her garden tools before the weather turned cold. As she wheeled the barrow into the shed, she caught sight of strange foliage behind the shed and went to investigate. Lo and behold, there in front of her was a flourishing honeydew patch with several fruit.

Now, how did this patch of honeydew come to be here? she wondered. This was an area that no one used. In fact, had she not found them when she did, Mrs. Townsend was certain the fruit would have perished. She picked the fully matured, evenly ripened fruit and used the barrow to transport them to the house, still wondering how they had come to be there.

That afternoon, as soon as he came in from school, Peter was drawn to the succulent fruit in the kitchen.

"Mom, where did you get all these delicious-looking honeydews?" he asked his mother.

"I was hoping you could tell me," his mother said, for she had been thinking long and hard about the origin of the honeydew patch.

She went on to explain where she had gotten the fruit, and she did not have to ask her son if he knew how the plants came to be behind the shed, because as she spoke, his face became bright red. He began to rub his hands together, and his eyes began to twitch. He was so ashamed, yet he was relieved to finally admit what he had done.

"I'm really sorry, Mom," he said. "That evening when I was supposed to take the basket of groceries to the Joneses, I did not take the whole honeydew to them. I ate a half and gave them only a half. I didn't want you to see the seeds in the garbage bins, so I buried them behind the shed. Then I forgot about them. I'm really sorry," he repeated.

The truth was, for some time now, Peter had secretly been agonizing about how to tell his mother what he had done. He had asked Jesus to forgive him long before, but he knew that even though he had tried to put the incident out of his mind, until he confessed to his mother he would not be comfortable. Now she knew and he felt much better. He stood before her, eyes downcast, awaiting his punishment.

His mother was silent for a while and then asked him, "How do you believe you should be punished for what you've done?"

He quickly said, "I'll do the dishes for two weeks!" He hated to do the dishes with the same intensity that he loved to eat honeydews.

"Fine," his mother said, adding "and I believe you should take some of these honeydews to the Joneses—half of them, in fact."

He eagerly nodded, then said, "I'll never do anything like that again, and to remind myself, I'm going to take a picture of these honeydews and have it printed and blown up and placed in my room."

He took his phone and quickly took a photograph of the honeydews. He also went outside and snapped the honeydew patch. As he did so, he looked up to the sky.

"Lord Jesus," he prayed, "I knew all along that You saw what I did and that it was wrong. I ask You again to forgive me and help me not to sin against You anymore. Thank you, Lord."

He went back to the house and braced himself to do the dishes.

Dear Friend, many times we forget that our heavenly Father sees and knows everything, even our thoughts. He says, "The heart *is* deceitful above all *things,*

And desperately wicked; Who can know it? I, the Lord, search the heart, I try the reins, even to give every man according to his ways, and according to the fruit of his doings. (Jer. 17:9, 10). Let us endeavor to make our God pleased by what He sees in us.

Gems:
There is so much good in the worst of us
And so much bad in the best of us
That it little become any of us
To speak ill of the rest of us

—Unknown, adapted

Think about it ...
If I did not love the Lord
And the Lord didn't love me,
Then, do you have any idea
Of just where I would be?

—K.V.A. St. A. Greenland

Changing Charlie

"Why doesn't Charlie like me?" Josh asked as he threw his books on the kitchen table.

His mom came in from the back porch. She approached him and gently tapped his hunched shoulder.

"Mom, I hate that school. I don't want to go back there. Charlie Jones is always picking on me," he wailed.

"Would you like me to go and talk with the teacher tomorrow?" Mrs. Smith asked.

"No, no, no!" her son said quickly. "The other kids will call me 'sissy' and 'momma's boy.'"

"So, how will we deal with this challenge?" his mother asked. There was silence for a while; then she said, "I know. The best way to get rid of an enemy is to change him into a friend. The next time Charlie tries to bother you, do your best to be nice to him."

"Mom, do you know what you're asking me to do? This guy's a monster! He'll hurt me!" Josh winced as he remembered how Charlie had twisted his arm that day.

"I know it won't be easy, Son, but you can do it. We'll ask Jesus to help you to do it. Remember what the Savior said as they crucified Him?"

"Father, forgive them, for they know not what they do," they both recited.[1]

"Well, I assure you, if you persist in being nice to Charlie, he will find it harder and harder to be mean to you," Mom said.

Josh knew his mother was usually right. There was the time she talked him into being friendly to the two dogs from next door, to stop them from barking at him every time he ventured outside. Then there was the time she convinced him that Mr. Livingston at the end of the street was really a nice old man instead of the old geezer Josh thought him to be. Well she had been right on those occasions, but he wasn't so sure she was this time.

"I, don't know Mom," he shook his head doubtfully, finally saying, "But ... I'll give it a try."

---

1 Luke 23:34.

Josh slept fitfully that night. He had a nightmare in which Charlie chased him, caught him, and used his shirt to tie him to the school's flagpole, then made the entire class pelt him with snowballs, even though it was the end of spring. He woke up shivering, more afraid than ever, and the extra hotdog his mom had put into his lunch box, so he could share it with Charlie, didn't make him feel any better.

I don't think this is going to be my day, he thought as he boarded the school bus.

The hours before lunch time seemed to fly. Josh spent most of them rehearsing what he would say to Charlie. Should he go straight to the bully or should he wait for Charlie to jump him as usual?

He didn't have to make that decision; for as he rounded the corner to enter the boys' washroom, Charlie lunged toward him, almost knocking him to the floor.

"Run! Run! There's a big cat in there!" Charlie shouted as he rushed down the corridor, still buttoning his pants.

Josh had visions of a huge lion or tiger and thought for a moment that he should also run. But then he heard a faint "meow" coming from the restroom and decided to investigate. There, on the floor, beside one of the booths, was a white-and-grey tabby. Josh had seen the cat on the school campus before, and he had tried to get her to go to him.

"Here, Kitty, Kitty, Kitty," he said. But the cat was not interested in him. She was staring at a small wooden box in one corner of the room. From the box peeked the tiny heads of four fluffy brown kittens. Josh made a step toward the box, and the mother cat raised herself to twice her height and hissed.

Now I see what Charlie meant when he said there was a big cat in here, he thought. He was not afraid of the cat, but he was not in a mood to be scratched. In any event, the thought of Charlie made him think of what his mom had asked him to do.

I wonder where he went, he thought as he walked toward the lunch room.

Charlie was sitting in his usual corner with a group of boys around him, and he was describing, in vivid detail, one of his run-ins with three boys from another school.

"I gave them such a whupping, they all ran home to their mamas," he ended, to much laughter.

Josh did not walk quietly to his seat in hopes that Charlie wouldn't notice him, as he would have done in the past. Instead, he strode purposefully toward Charlie's table, and the self-acclaimed boxing and karate champion suddenly looked defeated. Josh realized that the overgrown boy who had struck so much fear into him in the past was now afraid of him.

For a moment Josh was minded to bring up the matter of the little cat in the boys' bathroom, but he thought better of it. Instead, he said, "Hey, Charlie, my mom sent this hotdog for you."

The other boy blinked, temporarily at a loss for words; then he said, "Oh, yes. My mom is out of town, and I know she gave your mom some money to fix lunch for me."

He grabbed the bag and started wolfing down the contents. His eyes pleaded with Josh not to contradict what he had said.

Whatever, Josh thought, shrugging inwardly, but it only then occurred to him that he had never seen Charlie eat anything except what he had taken from other students.

"Mom also said you could come and have dinner at our house this evening," Josh said, fully aware that his mother would disapprove of his not telling the truth, but also trusting that she would welcome the opportunity to have Charlie visit her home.

I'll make sure to call her before we go back to class, he thought.

"Of course you can have him over," Mrs. Smith said, "But remember, I go to the women's Bible study at church this afternoon, so you'll be on your own for about half an hour before Dad gets home. As usual, Mrs. Thompson will look in on you."

In a few hours, the school bus dropped both boys near Josh's house, and right away Josh noticed that Charlie was very unsure of himself. He wondered whether taking Charlie home was a good idea, especially since his mother wouldn't be there. Well, it was now too late to have second thoughts.

"My parents are looking forward to meeting you," he told Charlie. "They'll be home soon. I'll just have to stop by our neighbor's and pick up the house key."

They got to the neighbor's house, and Josh opened the gate and entered the yard. Although he hadn't said so, he had expected Charlie to wait on the curb for him. He was therefore surprised to find the other boy following behind him.

Josh didn't have time to warn Charlie that Mrs. Thompson had two very mischievous dogs that would chase him just for fun, because right then, the two dogs rushed from behind the house. However, the dogs were not interested in Charlie. They were chasing a very scared stray cat that was darting this way and that, trying desperately to lose the dogs. On spotting the boys, the cat headed straight for Charlie.

Josh knew that the cat would try to climb up to his or Charlie's head to escape from the dogs.

"Duck, Charlie! Duck! Get low!" he shouted, as he stooped to the ground. But Charlie wasn't listening. He stood transfixed, a look of complete horror on his face as the cat narrowed the distance between them, with the dogs in hot pursuit.

There was only one thing that Josh could do. He hurled himself at the other boy and knocked him down onto the soft grass, while the cat, robbed of its refuge, swerved again and made a running leap over the fence.

Charlie lay breathless for several moments, then slowly sat up. His face and eyes glowed as he gazed at Josh.

"Man, you saved my life! You saved my life! Thank you! Thank you! Thank you!" he gasped.

"It's nothing!" Josh said, wondering if this was the same guy he had been so afraid of.

He collected the key, and soon they were inside his house.

After they washed their hands, Josh put their meals in the microwave oven, and soon they were eating. As before, Charlie ate like a starving man, but in between the gulps, he praised Josh.

"Man, you're my hero! You're a great guy! I'm gonna be your friend forever!"

"That's all right," Josh said, adding, "I'll be your friend, too, but there is one thing you'll have to promise me."

"What? What? Anything you say, man, anything!" Charlie gushed.

"Charlie, promise me that you will never again hurt people who are smaller than you are," Josh said.

"I'm really sorry about how I treated you in the past. I won't ever do those things again, to you or anyone," Charlie promised.

"Well, in that case, I'll always be there to save you from all the cats in the world," Josh said with a wink.

"Let's shake on that," Charlie said. And they did.

Dear Friend, especially my young friend, regardless of what you may hear some people say, it is not cool to be cruel to others, especially if they are smaller and weaker than you are. It doesn't matter if someone has been mean to you or if someone more powerful than you is picking on you. You should not lash out at those who are not able to defend themselves. And guess what, there is Someone who loves you and cares about what happens to you. He wants the best for you and wants you to do the right things. His name is Jesus, and He is willing and ready to forgive you for all the wrong things you've done, if you would only ask His forgiveness. Jesus says, "Him that cometh to Me I will in no wise cast out" (John 6:37).

If you are the one being bullied, don't be afraid to talk to someone you trust. Many times people will hurt others because they themselves are hurting. Sometimes the person who is bullying you is being bullied by someone else.

Although it is very difficult, try to be kind to a bully. Remember, Christ showed us that meekness is not weakness when, although with a word, He could have destroyed all those who wanted to kill him, He *allowed* Himself to be crucified. Solomon advises us, "A soft answer turneth away wrath; but grievous words stir up anger" (Prov. 15:1). And the best way to get rid of an enemy is to turn him into a friend.

Nature
God made the earth, the flowers, the trees.
He made little animals; you, me; the breeze
Whatsoever He created, He said it was good,
And He made all fruits so we could use them as food.

The flowers are beautiful as far as I can see,
And it's so good they were made for you and me.
The trees, too, are worthy of mention;
They are a part of God's wonderful creation.

It was out of delight that He made all the animals,
Such as little fishes and even the sea mammals.
He made other creatures from His mind above
As a gift to us, sent down with love.

But sin entered the world and took the joy we had,
Destroying God's natural beauty, also making Him sad.
Because of sin we were destined to die;
That's why God sent His Son—to save you and I.

—*K.V.A. St. A. Greenland*

A Rhyme
Here is a little rhyme that is 100 percent true.
There is a story of a man named Jesus
And what He came to do.
Now, the rhyme includes everybody
And everything, including the old and the new;
And for this purpose only
I share this rhyme with you.

—*K.V.A. St. A. Greenland*

Listening to the Holy Spirit

I have many things to say unto you, but ye cannot bear them now. Howbeit when He, the Spirit of Truth is come, He will guide you into all truth: for He shall not speak of Himself; but whatsoever He shall hear, that shall He speak: and He will shew you things to come. He shall glorify Me: for He shall receive of Mine, and shall shew it unto you.—John 16:12–14.

Sister Prudence Burke was always eager to share her faith and to introduce others to her Savior. After work most days, she would walk through her neighborhood, distributing pieces of religious literature and trying to sign-up candidates for Bible study.

Prudence was on one such mission one day. She knocked on the gate of a home in an area she had not visited before. A little girl, about nine years old, came through the front door of the house and approached her. Prudence greeted her and requested to speak with her parents.

"My parents do not live here," the little girl said, adding, "I live with my grandmother, but she said she is busy right now and asked that you leave a message."

Prudence quickly took two tracts from her bag, one for the girl and one for the adult, and gave them to the girl. She explained that she would like to study the Bible with them and asked the girl to ask her grandmother if she would be willing to allow her to do that. It took a long while and several trips back and forth by the little girl, whose name was Cindy; but finally, Prudence got what she wanted. The grandmother agreed that Prudence and her Bible study partner could visit her home the following Tuesday, five days hence, to begin to study the Bible with her and her grandchild.

"Grandma said to make sure not to come before seven o'clock in the evening, as we might not be home before then," Cindy added.

While all of this was going on, Prudence had the time to make a few observations. The small lawn in the small front yard needed cutting, and the tiny hibiscus hedge needed trimming. The exterior of the house badly needed a coat of paint, and from what she could see of the interior, the house was very scantily furnished. She also noticed that the young girl wore nothing on her feet as she raced from the gate to the house and back.

Being extremely kind and maternal, Prudence began to think of all the favors she could get done for this family. She would ask her husband to come by with his mower and hedge clippers and the give the front yard a makeover. She would ask one of her fellow church members, a painter, if he would paint the house, outside and most likely inside, free of cost, if she would provide the paint. She also knew that she was going to purchase some clothes and shoes for the little girl. All these things she decided would be done as soon as they all got to know one another a little better.

The five days flew by fast. Prudence and her prayer and Bible study partner prepared their lessons and prayed for divine guidance. On the Tuesday evening, as arranged, they met at seven o'clock about four blocks from the home and began walking toward the home. They passed several shops on the way, and as they walked and talked, the sun began to set. Soon darkness settled around them. Then Prudence developed a frown.

"What's the matter?" her friend asked.

"I don't know," Prudence said, putting her hand to her head. "I keep getting the impression that I am to go into the store and purchase a lamp wick.

"A lamp wick? What on earth for?" her friend laughed. "You have no lamp. What would you be doing with a lamp wick?"

Prudence couldn't answer that question. She only knew that she had an overwhelming urge to go into the store and purchase the wick for a lamp that runs on kerosene oil. The urge was so strong that at the last shop they passed before getting to their destination, Prudence stopped and tried hard to think of why she would want to purchase a lamp wick. Although several persons, especially in the rural parts, still used kerosene lamps to light their homes at night, Prudence could not think of anyone who did; and even though most persons who had electricity in their homes also had a back-up kerosene lamp, she didn't know anyone who needed a wick for their lamps, and she certainly did not need one herself.

Prudence felt that the Holy Spirit was urging her, but she questioned why she had to purchase a lamp wick of all things. She just could not make sense of such instruction.

With great effort, Prudence finally tore herself away from the front of the shop, despite how compelled she felt to go in and purchase a lamp wick, and they walked the remaining yards to the little house—somewhat faster now, as they had wasted precious minutes as she stopped in front of the store.

The first thing Prudence noticed as she approached the house was that while all the surrounding homes were well lit, it was in darkness. At first, she thought that older lady and her ward were still not home. As she stood at the gate wondering if she should wait a while, she heard a voice from the front of the house saying, "Is that you, Miss Burke?"

She quickly answered, "Yes, yes. I'm here with my partner, as I promised, to study the Bible with you." Then she asked, "But why are you sitting in the dark?"

The older woman sighed and replied, "The power company came and disconnected my electricity today. I wasn't even home when they did. I got home just before it became dark, and when I discovered there was no electricity, I decided to use my kerosene lamp, but then I recalled that the wick was all burnt out. I really have no money to purchase a wick right now, so Cindy and I are going to have to remain in the dark tonight. And I'm sorry, but we'll have to put off the Bible study until another time."

Prudence let out a wail as hot tears flooded her eyes and rushed down her cheeks.

"No! No! No! This can't be happening!" she cried.

The grandmother became quite alarmed, as she thought that Prudence was overreacting to the news that they could not have the Bible study.

It took quite a lot of explaining on the part of her friend—since Prudence was incoherent—for the lady to understand why she was so upset.

"I am disappointed that we cannot begin the Bible study," Prudence said when she finally calmed down, adding, "But that is not why I'm so upset. I am painfully aware of the fact that I have disobeyed the promptings of the Holy Spirit, and as a result, I have let Him down by not bringing the honor and glory that He deserves, to Him, for only He could have known that you would need the lamp wick and He chose me to get the wick and take it to you, and I failed! I failed!" she wailed, close to tears once more.

Even though Prudence was very distraught, the lady was sufficiently impressed by the incident. She assured them that she would get the electricity reconnected in a few days. Prudence insisted that she had to pay for the wick, so she accepted the price of the wick, ensuring that for the next few nights they would have some light in the house.

Prudence and her friend prayed for the little family, then took their leave after it was agreed that they would return the following Tuesday. It was a very subdued Prudence who walked the several blocks to her house, and that night, long after her family had retired, she agonized with the

Lord over her resistance to the Holy Spirit. She prayed and beseeched the Lord's forgiveness and promised never again to be so stubborn to His promptings. And she never was!

Dear Friend, the Holy Spirit is here to guide and instruct us in righteousness. It can be such a beautiful experience when we listen to and obey His instructions; for He always leads us aright. Let us endeavor to heed that "still small voice," and even when we don't understand why He wants us to do certain things, once we ascertain that it is His voice we hear, let us obey Him. As Samuel said to Saul, "Hath the LORD as great delight in burnt offerings and sacrifices, as in obeying the voice of the Lord? Behold, to obey is better than sacrifice and to harken than the fat of rams" (1 Sam. 15:22).

What Next?
O Lord I don't know what to do.
Once again I've broken my promise to You.
You told me to follow Your steps day by day,
But instead I treaded in my own selfish way.

O Lord, I want to be so much like You;
I want to be among the heaven-bound few.
I know that without You I'm nothing;
It seems so often that's what I keep forgetting.

Although I must surrender all for which I care,
I might still be left out—this is my fear.
It seems so hard, of earthly possession to let go,
But I can do it with Your help; that's what I know.

— *K.V.A. St. A. Greenland*

Sermon: *"Remember Lot's Wife"*

by Victor Greenland

Scripture Reading: Luke 17:26–32
Opening Hymn: #368, "Watchman, Blow the Gospel Trumpet"

    Today we must be in obedience to our Lord and Savior Jesus Christ as He commands to "Remember Lot's wife."
    Why has Jesus singled out Mrs. Lot as a woman for us to remember, and what might be the lesson for us in the memory of Lot's wife?
    Turn your Bibles to Genesis 11:27. It reads: "Now these are the generations of Terah: Terah begat Abram, Nahor, and Haran; and Haran begat Lot."
    So, Lot first came to our notice on the pages of Scripture in Genesis 11:27 as the son of Haran, the nephew of Abram and the grandson of Terah.
    In Genesis 11:31, 32, we read that Abram took Lot and the rest of his family from Ur of the Chaldees to the land of Canaan. It is not clear at this point whether Lot was married or not. They came to Haran and dwelled there for a while, and then Terah, Abram's father, died there at the ripe, old age of 205 years.
    In Genesis 12:1–4 we read that the Lord had said unto 75-year-old Abram,

> Get thee out of thy country, and from thy kindred, and from thy father's house, unto a land that I will shew thee: And I will make of thee a great nation, and I will bless thee, and make thy name great; and thou shalt be a blessing: And I will bless them that bless thee, and curse him that curseth thee: and in thee shall all families of the earth be blessed.

And Abram obeyed right away.

It could very well be that Lot met his wife and got married in Haran. One thing is certain: he got married and had children. Jesus reminds us in Luke 17:32, "Remember Lot's wife."

In Genesis 13, we read that after they left Haran, they experienced a famine. Abram, Lot, and Sarai went with their substance into Egypt. By then, Abram was very rich in cattle, silver, and gold. Lot was also quite wealthy. He had flocks and herds and tents. A quarrel soon developed between Lot's herdsman and Abram's herdsmen because the land could not support their animals as well as those of the Canaanites and Perizzites, who also dwelled in the land.

> Out of that quarrel we have the famous declaration by Abram to Lot:
> Let there be no strife, I pray thee, between me and thee, and between my herdmen and thy herdmen; for we be brethren. Is not the whole land before thee? Separate thyself, I pray thee, from me. If thou wilt take the left hand, then I will go to the right; or if thou depart to the right hand, then I will go to the left. (Gen. 13:8, 9)

Lot chose the well-watered plain of Jordan, which just happened to be near Sodom and Gomorrah. Notice that he pitched his tent *toward* Sodom. This one statement implies a great deal of danger. This means that Lot and his family daily had to witness the wickedness of Sodom. Genesis 13:13 tells us, "But the men of Sodom were wicked and sinners before the LORD exceedingly." "In Sodom there was mirth and revelry, feasting and drunkenness. The vilest and most brutal passions were unrestrained. The people openly defied God and His law and delighted in deeds of violence. Though they had before them the example of the antediluvian world, and knew how the wrath of God had been manifested in their destruction, yet they followed the same course of wickedness" (Patriarchs and Prophets, Chapter 14, p. 157). Ezekiel 16:49 tells us, "This was the iniquity of ... Sodom, pride, fullness of bread, and abundance of idleness."

But remember Lot's wife.

By associating with Sodom, Lot got his family in trouble in more ways than one. Gen 14:1, 2, tells us that Amraphel, king of Shinar; Arioch, king of Ellasar; Chedorlaomer, king of Elam; and Tidal, king of nations made war against Bera, king of Sodom; Birsha, king of Gomorrah; Shinab, king

Sermon: "Remember Lot's Wife"

of Admah; Shemeber, king of Zeboiim; and the king of Bela, which is Zoar. Apparently by then, Lot may have lived in Sodom. He was certainly near enough for his goods and his entire household to be taken captive when Sodom was overrun and its king defeated.

Like the good kinsman he was, Abram went to Lot's rescue and re-captured all his goods and his women and his people.

And he brought again his brother Lot, and his goods, and the women also, and the people. It still did not occur to Lot that he was living dangerously by remaining in Sodom.

But remember Lot's wife.

In Genesis 18, while Abram dwelled in Mamre, the Lord made a disclosure to him. By then, God had changed Abram's name to Abraham. The Lord told Abraham that the wickedness of Sodom and its sister city, Gomorrah, had become intolerable and that He would destroy the cities.

And the Lord said, *"Because the cry of Sodom and Gomorrah is great, and because their sin is very grievous; I will go down now, and see whether they have done altogether according to the cry of it, which is come unto me; and if not, I will know"* (Gen. 18:20, 21).

In the life of every city, there is the *year* of visitation, there is the *day* of visitation, and then there is the *hour* of visitation. It was now the *day* of visitation for Sodom and Gomorrah.

Realizing that Lot and his family lived in the area, Abraham pleaded with God to save the cities if a significant number of righteous persons could be found there. The number moved from fifty to ten. God promised to spare Sodom and Gomorrah if He could find 10 righteous persons in the two cities.

Abraham pleaded for righteous in Sodom, much like Jesus is now pleading for the righteous upon earth today.

Soon, it might be the day of visitation for the city in which you live.

So remember Lot's wife.

When the two messengers sent from heaven arrived in Sodom and Gomorrah, Lot, by virtue of his position, was able to greet them. Lot sat in the gate of Sodom, meaning he was one of the leaders of this city. He knew all that was happening in the city, so immediately he was fearful for the men.

We all know the story. He prevailed upon them to enter his house and remain there for the night because he dreaded what might happen to them if they remained in the streets. But the men had a specific mission, so they convinced Lot that the two cities would shortly be destroyed, because, of course, they had not found ten righteous souls. They urged Lot, his wife, and their two daughters to flee.

This is where Mrs. Lot comes in. Even though we are not told much about this lady, there are certain things we can deduce.

Mrs. Lot was a virtuous woman. Proverbs 31:10–31 gives us the attributes of a virtuous woman, and verse 23 says, "Her husband is known in the gates, when he sitteth among the elders of the land."

Mrs. Lot feared the Lord and had raised her children in the nurture and admonition of the Lord. She had stretched out her hands to the poor and reached forth her hand to the needy.

Why, then, does our Savior warn us to "remember Lot's wife"?

Mrs. Lot's problem was that she compromised a bit too much. She either acquiesced or was the leader when the suggestion was made that the family move to Sodom. She had witnessed the wickedness of the cities but rationalized that God would protect her family wherever they were. She had seen the strict standards by which she had raised her girls being eroded as the older ones followed the ways of their husbands, but she kept silent.

Therefore, on that fateful night when the angels told Lot to go and call his married daughters and his sons-in-law, she was devastated but not surprised by the young men's reaction and the fact that the daughters opted to stay with their husbands even after hearing their father's dire warnings.

The fact is that even as the angels caught hold of the hands of Lot, his wife, and their daughters, telling them not to look back, Mrs. Lot was overcome with regret about the opportunities she had neglected to impress upon the minds of her daughters and sons-in-law, the importance of serving God, giving glory only to Him, and of coming out of Sodom and Gomorrah literally and psychologically.

Therefore, when our Savior admonishes us to remember Lot's wife, He is talking to everyone who names the name of Christ. Are we using every opportunity we have now, while it is still day, to live a life of example for our children, relatives, and acquaintances? Are we too much in awe of our children and their worldly achievements that we are afraid to impress upon them their need to assume the humility of Christ? Have we allowed our children to get to the point where Christianity is no longer relevant or credible?

If we have, the good thing is that *there is still time*. Let us now impress upon all those we know, especially our children, that

> Now it is high time to awake out of sleep: for now is our salvation nearer than when we believed. The night is far spent, the day is at hand: let us therefore cast off the works of darkness, and let us put on the armour of light. Let us walk honestly, as in the day; not in rioting and drunkenness, not in chambering and wantonness, not in strife and envying. But put ye on the Lord Jesus Christ, and make not provision for the flesh, to fulfil the lusts thereof. (Rom. 13:11–14)

Remember Lot's wife.

Closing Hymn: #600, "Hold Fast Till I Come"

The Evangelist Dog

Mabel and Johnathan Harry had been married for twenty-nine years. They had raised three beautiful children and, from all outward indications, had had a wonderful life together.

There was something, however, that ate at Mabel's heartstrings: something that gave her many sleepless nights, something about which she prayed and agonized almost all of the time she was awake and dreamed about almost all the time she slept.

Johnathan, a loving and caring husband and father, was not a Christian. They had talked about becoming Christians thirty-two years before, when they courted. They had both started attending church, but when the time came for them to make a commitment to Christ, while Mabel eagerly accepted Him as Lord of her life, Johnathan hesitated. And even though he dutifully accompanied her to church for several years after they married, and his presence was most helpful while the children were small, Mabel knew that he did it just to please her.

Sadly, the time came when, because of demands at work and various other social responsibilities he had undertaken, Johnathan began to make excuses about going to church.

First it was just to stay home and sleep. "I'm too tired this morning," he would groan. "If I come, I'm going to spend the whole time nodding, and you know how much I hate to see people sleeping in church."

So Mabel would get her children ready, bundle them into the family's comfortable sedan, and drive the one and a half miles to church, outwardly cheerful but inwardly weeping and pleading with the Lord for her husband. On the first number of occasions that Johnathan stayed home, they would return at the end of the Sabbath to find Johnathan well rested and in a great mood, ready to take the family out for a treat. Increasingly often, however, they would return to an empty house and find a note of apology. "They had an emergency at the plant and there was nobody else to deal with it. Sorry. I'll be back as soon as I can. Love you all."

Then the arguments started. "John, you have been a great provider for this family, and I know how important your job is to you, but don't you think that working on the Sabbath is taking things a bit too far?"

"Who's working on the Sabbath? Am I working on the Sabbath?"

"But sometimes you spend all day at the plant."

"Can I help it if a machine breaks down and I'm the only one available who can fix it? Didn't Jesus say if your donkey falls into a pit on the Sabbath, you are to pull it out? Well, my fixing the machine is equivalent to that."

"First of all, Jesus didn't say that. In Luke 14:5 He asked the lawyers and Pharisees which of them, if their donkey were to fall into a pit, would leave it there because it was the Sabbath. He knew, and they knew, that they would quickly have acted to save their beast, yet they objected to His *healing a person* on the Sabbath. But what you have to work with are not live creatures. They won't die because no one is available right away to fix them when they break down. Thirdly, you are not the only person available to fix the machine. They just know that if they call you, you will go."

"Of course, I'm going to go. I have to safeguard my livelihood and your interest and the children's future. If the company has too much down time, they will have to cut the benefits they give. They might even have to cut jobs. At my age, I am not going to start over at another company. I have invested too much in this one already."

"I am not saying your job is not important. I'm saying that keeping the Sabbath holy is more important. I'm concerned about your laying up treasure for yourself on earth and forgetting that nothing down here will last. Even if you're not working, you can't keep the Sabbath holy if you spend the whole day amid a group of smoking, drinking, carousing people who are not careful about what they say."

"Well, perhaps if ... your church didn't go on for the entire day, I could go to the service and still have time to help out at the plant."

Mabel could not believe what she was hearing! "Johnathan Harry! You know that's a most unfair thing to say. You know that God says He gives us six days, six out of seven, to labor and do all *our* work, but He requires that for one day, just twenty-four hours, we forget about the hustle and bustle of everyday life and concentrate on His goodness and mercy toward us. Is that too much?"

Johnathan felt it was too much, but he dared not say so. By now, Mabel's voice had risen a few decibels and she was perilously close to tears. He hated upsetting his wife but failed to see why she was making such a fuss about his missing church. It wasn't as if he had gotten anything out of the services on the occasions he did go.

There would be times when the children, especially the two girls, would add their voices to their mother's pleadings. "Daddy, please, pretty please, come back to church with us. It is so awkward when it's Fathers' Day or Men's Day and we don't have you at church." He would always promise them that he would soon be going.

Sometimes he would even name a particular Sabbath on which he would be going, but something would always come up, something urgent that would prevent him from going, and he could not understand why his family refused to see that it was not his fault. He soon began to think that they, especially his wife, were a bit selfish. They only saw things from their own perspective. Although he tried to be as loving and attentive as before, he felt a tension build between him and his family. Family time would always be spoiled by someone bringing up the subject of his relationship with Christ and how he spent his Saturdays. He soon became very subdued at home, afraid to start an argument in which he was on one side and everybody else was against him.

Mabel ached for the closeness they had before the arguments started, but she also knew she had a responsibility to point out his failings. She intensified her pleading with the Lord on her husband's behalf and was so grateful that her children each chose to follow the Lord and, of their own volition, had committed their lives to Him. In their daily devotions they never failed to lift Johnathan up in prayer, and Mabel even asked a few of her trusted friends at church to place him on their prayer lists.

✳✳

Years passed. The children were grown and gone. Although she spoke with them daily and visited them as often as she could, Mabel still suffered from the empty nest syndrome. With the children out of the house, she and Johnathan made an effort to recapture the romance in their earlier lives. For their thirtieth anniversary they went for an extended cruise in the Caribbean on which they had some real soul-searching discussions and vowed to draw even closer to each other.

Mabel had by now ceased to talk to him about committing to the Lord, though she never failed to mention him every time she went down on her knees. He had gotten to the point where he would not leave the house on the Sabbath, but he was still adamant about not going to church.

"I can stay right here and worship God," he would say, adding, "In any event, I do not want to associate with all those hypocrites who are so righteous in church but are devils outside."

For Mabel's fifty-fifth birthday, the children gave her a beautiful beagle. Even though she was not too keen about having a pet, Mabel soon learned that Mr. Tibs, as she named him, was just what she needed to satisfy her mothering instinct.

Soon the pair was inseparable. They would go for long walks, go to the store together, go to visit shut-ins, even distribute evangelistic literature. Then, for some reason, Mabel felt compelled to take Tibs along with her when she went to prayer meetings. The little dog would curl up under her pew and would remain there for the entire service. Eventually, everyone got accustomed to his presence, and if they didn't see him, they would ask Mabel where he was. Eventually, he was also accompanying her to Sunday night service, and finally, he would spend the entire Sabbath at church. He acted as if he fully understood the pastor's sermons, and interestingly, he was noticeably better behaved than some of the children and even some older ones.

At home Mabel developed the habit of talking to Tibs about her faith, even when Johnathan was around. He couldn't really accuse her of targeting him, because he knew that this was how she talked to the dog all the time. Often he had come home and entered the house quietly to find Tibs paying rapt attention, listening to Mabel read the Bible or explain a point or simply praise the Lord for some victory she had won.

Johnathan tolerated the aberration because it seemed to make Mabel happy, and after her little service was complete, she would place the dog in his cage and become the loving attentive wife she had always been.

In this way they passed several more years. Johnathan rose to become CEO at his company and, "of necessity," had to attend a few functions on the Sabbath. He went alone. Then eventually, he retired and for the first time in many years, they had another argument about the Sabbath. The company decided to hold his farewell function on a Sabbath eve, and he did not see any reason to ask them to reschedule it for another time. Well, Mabel did not see any reason for her to attend and break the Sabbath, so he went alone, and he was furious!

This last decision by Mabel seemed to make Johnathan even more hardened against the church and against God; and even as she prayed earnestly that God would soften and enlighten him, she was positive that she had done the right thing.

As it turned out, Johnathan had to quickly abandon his anger. One night, shortly after he went on retirement, Mabel fell seriously ill.

For a few months previously, she had been troubled by severe headaches and dizzy spells and been receiving treatment for migraine. This particular night the pain was blinding, and she alternated between blessed oblivion and absolute agony.

At one point, she knelt down by her side of the bed to pray, and Johnathan listened intently as his wife, with a strangled voice, pleaded with God for relief. Slowly, her words became softer and slower until they stopped altogether. Johnathan waited for her to rise from her knees. Two minutes went by. Five minutes went by.

"She must be saying things she doesn't want me to hear," he thought, propping himself up on his arms and looking at her intently.

He noticed then that there was a frightening stillness about her. Alarmed, but not wanting to show it, he gently placed his hand on her head.

"Moms," he said, gently. There was no answer.

"Mabel!" he almost shouted, and shook her. No answer.

The EMS was quickly called, and Mabel was whisked to the emergency room of the local hospital.

Johnathan put calls through to his children and relatives and followed the ambulance to the hospital. As he paced the corridors waiting for some news about his wife, for the first time in his life Johnathan felt completely alone, so alone; he felt like crying. Suddenly, he could hear Mabel's voice saying to Tibs, "Remember you are never alone. God is always with you." He remembered one of the songs she was always singing. "God is always near me, hearing what I say …." Then he distinctly heard her saying gently to him, "Why don't you pray, John? God will hear you." He heard that admonition over and over as he watched the medical personnel hurrying to and fro in their professional, detached manner.

"Well. God, it's a good thing that she is the one who is ill and not me, because if I was the one lying on that bed, I would not be talking to you, for I'm not sure you would want to hear from me. But she is yours. She has served you with all her heart all her life. Don't let her suffer so." He broke off as he saw a group of people whom he vaguely recognized

The Evangelist Dog

coming toward him. It was a group from Mabel's church. Where were they going? How did they know …?

"My dear brother, we just heard that Sister Mabel was taken here. Your children called and told us. Please be assured that the church is praying right now, and we've come over to see if there is anything we can do." This was from the head deacon of the church, Tom Anderson.

Johnathan didn't have much to tell them. They knew about the headaches and fainting spells she had been having. This was one of those episodes, but much worse. He didn't think there was anything they could do. They didn't have to wait around. He would inform them if there were any changes.

The fact was, he was always uncomfortable in the presence of these people, even when he used to attend church. He always had the impression they could see right through him and they saw the emptiness he had inside. Besides, he just didn't want them to see how vulnerable he was at this time. He was too close to tears.

"Well, if you are sure there is nothing we can do here, we'll leave. But we want to say a word on your behalf before we leave. Before Johnathan could quite fathom the words, the group had formed a tight circle around him, and three of them offered short prayers for his family. Johnathan hardly heard the words, but he thought it strange that his name was mentioned far more often than Mabel's, and he remembered that each person ended his prayer with "nevertheless not our will, but Thy will, be done."

It seemed like an eternity after they left that Johnathan was finally allowed to see Mabel. She had been heavily sedated but was still in severe pain, yet she had a peaceful expression as she gazed into the eyes of her husband. "John, please take care of yourself and the children and Mr. Tibs," she said softly. "Remember, God loves you, John. God loves you and He wants you to …," she said, drifting off into sleep.

Johnathan wondered if the drugs had made her forget that the children were no longer at home and that he, therefore, did not need to be taking care of them, at least not for the short period she would be hospitalized. Certainly, Tibs needed his care, and Johnathan was glad that the house would not be completely empty when he returned home.

He spoke with the doctor after he left her room. He didn't like what he heard.

"Mr. Harry, we want to run some more tests. There may be an occlusion in the brain, but we're reasonably sure it's not caused by an embolism. We'll know definitely after the tests."

Johnathan was only too eager to give whatever permission was needed for the medical team to do their job. He just wanted his wife better.

As if he knew it was his duty to be up, even though it was close to 3:00 a.m., Tibs was waiting in anticipation when Johnathan finally returned home.

"Well, boy, it's you and me for now," he said, absentmindedly patting the dog's head. "Your mama has been admitted to the hospital, but she's gonna be all right. She's gonna be all right. She's gonna be all right." He kept repeating this, more to reassure himself than the dog. The fact was, he dared not encourage any other thought, for he could see no life for himself without his Mabel at his side. With that thought, sitting in Mabel's favorite chair, in the living room, his hand resting gently on the dog's head, Johnathan drifted off into an uneasy sleep.

The shrill ring of the telephone startled him, and for a moment he wondered why Mabel wasn't answering it. Then realization hit him. It could be the hospital! Could it be that ...? He sprang from the chair and dashed for the receiver. "Hello? Hello?"

"Hi, Dad. It's me, Marjorie. How are you?"

Johnathan was so overwhelmed to hear the voice of his elder daughter, he almost broke down. "I am holding up," he said, bravely. "But it's your mom I'm worried about. She is suffering so," his voice trailed off.

"Believe me, Dad, Mom is okay. She knows that there is no suffering we can experience in this world that even remotely compares to the joy that will be ours in the hereafter. Besides, Jesus suffered much more."

Johnathan could feel resentment rising within him at the obvious platitudes she was quoting. She really was Mabel's child, for her mother would have said the same thing. He could find nothing civil to respond with, so he remained silent.

"Dad, are you still there? Mom is okay," she repeated. "It's you I'm worried about, because if God wills that Mom should die, I know it will be just a sleep for her. I'm sure she will be in the first resurrection, never to suffer or die again. And we would not despair, for we know that we will be with her in eternity. But Dad," his daughter's voice lowered and became sad, pleading, "the one thing that will make my mother sad, if she were to die now, is the knowledge that she may never see her dear husband again."

Johnathan was near to tears now. He was livid but wasn't sure whether he was more angry with himself or with her. He felt an acute sense of failure and inadequacy, because here was a human being he had helped to produce and raise who was enunciating a topic with information he could neither confirm nor refute. He had no idea what she was talking about and did not know how to respond.

He tried bravado. "Look, all of this is highly unnecessary. Your mother is going to be fine. She'll be back home in a few days," he said a little impatiently.

"Okay, Dad. I'll change the subject," she said. "I was really calling to tell you we'll all be there for the weekend. It took a little effort, but we were all able to arrange time off, so prepare for a home invasion."

Again Johnathan felt uneasy. With his three children and their spouses—all practicing Christians—and the grandchildren in the house over the weekend, the discussion was invariably going to turn to religion. But the loving father he was, he would be delighted to have them home.

"Thank you, Pumpkin," he said, and she soon rang off.

Johnathan was now wide awake, so he set about mechanically doing the tasks that Mabel would have done had she been at home: watering the plants, indoors and outdoors, taking Tibs for his necessary walk, fixing them both something to eat. Mr. Tibs had worked up an appetite from his walk and enthusiastically dug into his meal. Johnathan pushed around the food on his plate until he was tired of the activity, and then he cleared the table.

A call to the hospital while he was preparing the meal had yielded no new information. "Mrs. Harry is still under sedation. She will be taken to the lab for the tests at 8:30," the nurse had told him. He calculated that the tests would last about two hours, so he planned to be at the hospital by 10:30. The problem was what to do with the intervening hours.

"You know, Tibs," he said to the dog as he moved listlessly around the house, Tibs in tow, "I remember the days when the minutes and hours moved too fast for me. In fact, it seems like yesterday. How come these minutes are so long?"

The little dog could only wag its tail and give him a look of sympathy. Again, Johnathan had an overwhelming sense of his own inadequacy and lack of control over events.

If Mabel were there, she would have some wise saying to fit the situation, but he could think of nothing to say; in fact, he could think of nothing. His mind had gone blank, and a dull sense of foreboding just hung over him.

Then, unmistakably, he heard Mabel's voice beside him. "Johnnie, why don't you pray? Jesus is waiting to comfort you." Normally, to Mabel, he was John. When she was annoyed with him, he was Johnathan. When she was particularly put out, he was Johnathan Harry. But when she wanted to be nice to him, he was Johnnie, and if she really wanted to get him to do exactly what she wanted, she could make her voice drip with honey when she said that name. This was the way he heard her speaking to him just now. "Please, Johnnie, do it for me, if not for yourself. Talk to the Savior."

Johnathan felt compelled to drop to his knees, but once there, he had no idea what to say. Well, as it turned out, he didn't have to say anything, for he was being spoken to. It was Mabel's voice he was hearing, but he knew that God was talking to him: *"When thou passest through the waters, I will be with thee; and through the rivers, they shall not overflow thee: when thou walkest through the fire, thou shalt not be burned; neither shall the flame kindle upon thee."* It was one of her favorite verses, taken from Isaiah 43, and Johnathan was amazed at the comfort those words brought him. Even after he arose from his knees, he could hear them repeated over and over, and he somehow obtained the strength he needed to get through the next two hours. Soon he was on his way to the hospital.

In fact, by the time he walked into the doctor's office, he was beginning to feel very optimistic. He was, therefore, not prepared for the somber look he saw on the doctor's face, nor for his words. "I'm very sorry, Mr. Harry, but …" The words came at him with deliberate, devastating effect. He did not hear all of them. He didn' t have to. The main point was that his wife was gravely ill. "There was no sign of this before … It is too far developed … brain tumor ... inoperable … a few months at most …"

"No! No! No! That cannot be!" He shouted and put his hand to his ears in an effort to ward off the verbal blows the doctor was dealing him. "My wife cannot die! She must not die!" he said, but this time his voice was much softer as he looked pleadingly at the doctor. "Isn't there another test … another doctor?"

"I'm very sorry, Mr. Harry," the doctor repeated. "We've already electronically transferred your wife's CT scans to our head hospital and to two of the leading neurosurgeons in this country. They have all confirmed our diagnosis and prognosis. An operation is out of the question. Its chances of success are non-existent. All we can offer now is some relief from the severe pain she will be enduring until the end comes ...," his said, his voice trailing off.

Johnathan had no idea how long he sat in the doctor's office. One part of him wanted to jump up and rush to Mabel's side. Another part wanted to run far away and hide, and yet another denied that any of this was happening. His wife was not terminally ill. This was all a bad dream from which he would awaken soon. He willed himself to stand, but his legs ignored him. He tried to speak but his throat was constricted and his jaws were locked. The doctor's lips were still moving, but all Johnathan could hear were the pounding of his own heart and the echo of the doctor's earlier words, "... until the end comes ... until the end comes ... until the end comes ... until the end comes"!

Finally, the doctor's lips stopped moving, and he stood to his feet. Johnathan shook his head furiously to break the spell that had overtaken him. He staggered to his feet and clung desperately to the edge of the doctor's desk. "What should I do now?" The voice startled him before he realized that it was his own.

"I have to go now, but Lawrence Lindsay will be here soon. He's already spoken to Mrs. Harry." The doctor fingered a chiming pager as he spoke, and Johnathan wished he had listened more keenly to what had been said to him.

"Does Mabel know all this?" he asked.

"Yes, Mr. Harry," the doctor replied. "Normally we would have waited to talk to the family first, but Mrs. Harry insisted that we confirm what she already suspected. She took the news remarkably calmly."

That's my Mabel, Johnathan thought, and asked, "Can I see my wife now?"

"Well, as I said, the hospital chaplain will be here any minute now to talk to you and your wife, if you so desire." Again the doctor apologized for the situation and looked relieved when a well-built, balding, middle-aged man with a sunny smile and kind, brown eyes knocked and entered the room. They quickly exchanged pleasantries. The doctor introduced the two men, then left.

Lawrence Lindsay went straight to the point. "Do you believe in God, Mr. Harry?"

"Are you asking if I believe He exists? Of course I do," Johnathan said, adding, "but if you're asking whether I have a relationship with Him, I'm afraid that answer is no. I have never had any time for God. I haven't really felt I needed Him, and now that I really need Him, I'm sure He isn't going to show any interest in me."

"But God is not like that at all, Mr. Harry. He doesn't bear grudges and is always a present help in trouble," the chaplain said.

"He is? Well, how come He is about to let my wife die—a woman who, I must say, has served Him faithfully? You tell me that!" He shouted the last bit, finding comfort in venting his anguish on someone.

For a while, the chaplain said nothing. He stood with his head bowed, and Johnathan suspected he was praying. Finally, he said, "We do not always understand what God does. But we know that all things work together for good to those who love the Lord—"

Johnathan interrupted him: "My wife loves the Lord, but show me how her suffering and death will be for her good."

"I can't tell you that now. I can only say that I believe it will work out not only for her good but for yours as well," Lawrence Lindsay said.

Johnathan formed another retort in his mind but thought better of its delivery as a vision of Mabel's disapproving look came to him. He sighed and his shoulders slumped. "Can we go to see my wife now, please?" he asked, meekly.

The chaplain agreed with alacrity, and they quickly crossed three hallways and entered Mabel's room. To Johnathan's surprise, there was a group of her fellow church members there, some of whom he had seen the previous night. Even the pastor was present. They seemed to have been having a jolly time while someone told an amusing story.

"Hi, Hon'," Mabel greeted her husband with outstretched arms. Her eyes searched his face to see how he had taken the news of her serious illness. The group parted to allow him to reach her side, and he wished desperately that they were alone so that he could take her in his arms and comfort her, or more truthfully, that she could comfort him.

A quick round of introductions was made. "Mabel, I shall have to finish my tale on my next visit." This was from a tall, lanky man with a toupee. Johnathan recalled that his name was Herb and that he had lost his wife six months earlier. Well, he certainly didn't look like someone who was grieving.

"Sister Mabel, we realize that your time is more precious now than ever, so we are not going to take up too much of it," said Pastor Nathan Brooks. "We'll just say a short word and leave, but we'll be back and we will not cease to pray for you and your family." He looked straight into

Johnathan's eyes as he said the last bit, and quickly three prayers were said, with the pastor saying the last one.

"Heavenly Father, we are in no doubt that You are in charge. We know You hold the future, and we are thankful that You also hold our hands. All is well that's done by Thee. So, Father, we will not presume to tell You what to do. We are confident that You will do what's best for us. You will do what's best for Sister Mabel and for her family. We only ask, Lord, that You give us the courage and the humility to accept what You do. Thank You, Lord. Amen. Now my dear brother and sister, we'll take our leave." He motioned with his head to the other church members, and they all said their farewell and started toward the door.

"Thank you all so much for coming," Mabel said cheerily.

You could almost believe they came over for afternoon tea and pleasantries, Johnathan thought sarcastically, but he desperately wished that that were the case. He also wished he could share the obvious optimism enjoyed by his wife and her friends.

The others having taken their leave, the chaplain, Johnathan, and Mabel spoke for a short while about the eventualities of the situation.

"I see you're in good hands, Mrs. Harry," he told Mabel. "So I'll be here only as back-up. Don't hesitate to call on me if you think I can be of assistance." Again he offered a short word of prayer and left.

Johnathan felt weak with relief when he was finally alone with his wife. There was so much he wanted to ask her, so much he wanted to say. Mabel forestalled him by placing her finger on his lips.

"Shh," she said, as if she could hear his thoughts. "Let's just enjoy each other in silence for a while." And that they did. Johnathan lost track of time as he sat on the edge of her bed, cradling Mabel's head on his knee while their entire life together flashed in front of him. Sometimes he winced at something stupid he had done, but more often, he smiled.

"Yeah, we've had a wonderful life together," he said softly and was surprised when Mabel did not respond. He then realized something that would become painfully obvious in the coming weeks, namely that Mabel, formerly indefatigable, now became tired after the slightest exertion. She was fast asleep.

After gently laying her head on her pillow, Johnathan sat by Mabel's bed for hours just watching her sleep and trying to etch every aspect of her features indelibly in his mind. Ever so often, a nurse or lab technician would come in and he would step outside the door and wander aimlessly up and down the corridor until he could enter again. Thus the day passed and the night passed. Then the following days and nights passed.

Johnathan now measured time by the occasions he was by, or away from, Mabel's bedside. The kids and their families came and went away; came again and went away again; and some of them returned and went away again. Other relatives, friends, and acquaintances came to visit and left. By then, Mabel had been moved back home and had a nurse with her around the clock. She was in severe pain most of the time and had to be heavily sedated, so she slept a lot.

On the odd occasion, however, she was the old, jovial Mabel, and on those occasions she would play with Mr. Tibs and speak to Johnathan about his soul's salvation. Johnathan still refused to have anything to do with God. In fact, while he had been apathetic toward God before, now he felt downright hostile.

"How can I approach a God who is bent on destroying my life?" he asked no one in particular. He had stopped pleading with God to let Mabel live and take him instead. He had now adopted a bravado that Mabel saw through right away. She used the last ounces of her strength to plead with God to give her husband the peace that she had found in Him, but she knew that Johnathan had to be willing to surrender, and she saw no sign of such surrender.

The end came suddenly. It happened on a weekend when all the children were visiting. Mabel had felt well enough to attend Sabbath school and morning service at her church, and of course, Mr. Tibs had gone along. After church and a wonderful Sabbath lunch, the family had cuddled up with her and told amusing stories. Everyone had a camera, and Johnathan jokingly accused them of being the paparazzi.

"Can we help if there is such a big celebrity around?" they all exclaimed and clicked away.

By sundown Mabel was exhausted but happy. As the family held a vespers service, Johnathan sat beside his wife and sang lustily. He bowed his head during the prayers and wished desperately that they were gathered under different circumstances. Later, as he kissed his wife good night, she squeezed him and said, "I love you, Johnnie Harry. Your children all love you, and," she said, pausing and then looking him in the eye with a serious expression on her face, "God loves you. He really loves you. And just because you don't understand what He is doing is no reason to distrust Him. Someday you'll understand it all."

For once, Johnathan didn't argue. Something told him not to. He simply rocked her gently in his arms until she settled into peaceful sleep.

At about 3:30 the next morning, Johnathan was awakened by a gentle rap on his door. It was Mabel's nurse. There was no need for words. He dressed quickly and rushed to his wife's side.

She looked as peaceful as she did when he had left her, but the nurse said, "She hasn't awakened since you left her, but an hour ago I took her vitals and found that they had slowed somewhat. I have been taking them every ten minutes since, and they continue to slow down." She showed Johnathan her chart.

It was obvious. Mabel was leaving them. He roused the children, and they all encircled her bed. They nestled up against her, cuddled her, hugged her, held her hands, even just touched her, trying desperately to convey the love they felt for her. She stirred and frequently smiled but did not open her eyes. They sang to her, spoke to her, prayed for her. Thus they spent the next two hours with her.

When Mabel exhaled for the last time, there were a few tears, especially from the grandchildren, but their parents reassured them that "one day soon we'll see Grandma again, and we'll all be together, forever."

Johnathan was the man of the moment. He knew his wife would have wanted him to be the support his children would lean on, and he was just that. Most of the final arrangements had already been made, so he was merely the facilitator, allowing things to fall into place.

They had a lovely memorial service for Mabel at her church. Of course, Mr. Tibs was in attendance. He and Johnathan sat as glowing accounts were given of Mabel's life. Johnathan tried not to be resentful, but as he looked around at all those in attendance, even his children, he thought about how they would all soon be returning to their homes to their unbroken family circles.

"When you think about it, Tibs, you and I are the only ones who will be without our loved one tonight," he mumbled to the little dog as they drove home later.

As it turned out, the house was almost empty that night, as most of the relatives and children who had exhausted their vacation time during Mabel's illness had to rush back to work and school. Their daughter Marjorie and son James stayed behind because they felt their father shouldn't be alone that night.

In the morning James, who had to return to his job that afternoon, tried to convince Johnathan to go and spend a few weeks—or days, even—with his family.

"Oh no! If I'm going to be alone for the rest of my life, I may as well start off right away," he said illogically. And there was nothing they could say to make him change his mind.

Marjorie stayed with him another week. With the help of some of Mabel's friends, she was able to sort out her mom's belongings and discard all but those that her father would not part with. She tidied the house and yard, made sure that there was enough food in the house to feed an army—of men and dogs—and got Johnathan to reluctantly agree to allow some of the ladies to check on him periodically.

"Dad, please do not hesitate to call if you get too lonesome. One of us will be here in a flash," she said as she kissed him goodbye.

"Don't mention that," he scolded her. "You and I both know that I won't have a chance to call. You'll all be here more often than I can stand to have you." They both laughed at that then grew serious and silent as thoughts of Mabel came to mind.

"You were one lucky man. Do you know that? To have had such a wonderful woman as your wife," she said.

"I'm still a lucky man, Pumpkin. I've got all her wonderful children to take care of me and to remind me of her every day. But don't you worry about me. Mr. Tibs will be good company. He nodded toward the little dog sitting at his feet. "And I know you're all just a phone call away."

With that assurance, Marjorie left, and for the very first time since that fateful morning when he learned of his wife's imminent death, Johnathan not only felt alone; he *was* alone. Everyone had left except for Tibs, of course, and Tibs needed to be fed; he needed to be taken for his walks; he needed to be groomed and spoken to. Johnathan was grateful for the therapeutic value of having to care for the dog, and he derived added pleasure from the knowledge that this was Mabel's own beloved pet.

He was determined, however, to have nothing to do with Mabel's friends, who were all members of her former church, and he certainly didn't want to have anything to do with her God. Whenever the ladies called or visited, he was polite but not friendly, making sure to let them know he was doing fine by himself.

For its part, the dog seemed to have accepted the loss of his mistress and adjusted to his new master. He was very understanding when

Johnathan overslept and he had to have his breakfast later than usual, or when Johnathan was too lazy to walk with him and just let him loose in the backyard.

One thing Tibs could not understand, however, was why his new master refused to go out with him one day each week to that nice place where all the kind people were. Of course, Tibs had no way of communicating his concerns to Johnathan—no way, that is, except to bark. Johnathan couldn't understand why Tibs never barked if he was not fed or bathed or walked on time for six days of the week but seemed particularly upset on a Saturday morning when he, like a caged animal, darted from one side of the house to the other and barked his head off. Even after he was fed and walked and groomed, he would still be restless.

One morning, not caring to hear another bark, Johnathan opened the back door and told Tibs to go and play in the yard. Within a few minutes, there was silence, and Johnathan settled in to read the sports page of the local newspaper. He must have fallen asleep, because he soon realized that it was past noon.

Where's Tibs? He must be hungry and thirsty, he thought as he scrambled to his feet and rushed to the door. He expected to see the little dog sitting patiently on the steps, waiting to be let back in. But Tibs was nowhere in sight. Johnathan called his name several times but got no response. That's strange, he thought. *That's not like Tibs. I'd better go and see where he could be.*

Well, he practically had nothing on, so he had to get his clothes and his shoes. By the time he got back to the door, he heard a faint yap on the other side and opened it to see Mr. Tibs sitting there with a smug look on his face.

"Where have you been? Don't you know you had me worried?" Johnathan asked, as if he expected a reply. When none was forthcoming, he ushered the little dog, and continued to fuss, inside. Tibs seemed contented to curl up and sleep after a hearty meal and then a long drink of water. He seemed none the worse for wear, so Johnathan forgot about his strange behavior.

The following Saturday morning, Tibs again threw a tantrum, and Johnathan shooed him outside. After a few minutes, all became quiet, and Johnathan decided to see what the little dog was up to. Tibs was nowhere to be seen. Johnathan called and called. Tibs did not respond.

I wonder if he has gone through the fence, he thought. He searched the fence but saw no opening. Then, maybe someone had opened the gate so the little dog could get out. But he found the gate securely fastened. Johnathan was at a complete loss. Where was Tibs? He didn't want to raise an alarm only to have the little dog turn up and make him look silly. He returned to the house, leaving the back door slightly ajar, and decided to wait a few hours at least before calling someone. Since there was nothing he wanted to do, he made himself comfortable on the couch and fell asleep.

He awoke to the distinct feeling that someone was watching him intently. He got up with a start and found Mr. Tibs sitting on his hind quarter, pink tongue hanging from his mouth, tail wagging slowly, just looking at him. Again, Johnathan began questioning the dog, who, of course, had nothing to say. He seemed fine, and he was hungry! After a huge meal, he curled up in his bed and went to sleep.

Johnathan realized that he was in the middle of a mystery, and he was determined to get to the bottom of it. The following Saturday morning, he let Tibs through the back door but was determined not to let him out of his sight. After running around the house a few times, Tibs sat quietly and stared at the house. Johnathan silently watched from behind the heavy curtains, and the little dog, apparently not perceiving that he was being watched, quickly went to a section of the fence in the corner of the yard that is near the road. He quickly dug a hole in the sand under the fence, then squeezed himself through the fence. Once on the other side, he scratched at the sand and blocked the hole. Then he darted down the road.

On inspecting the spot, Johnathan was surprised at how effectively the dog had covered the hole. *That's the reason I didn't see the hole when I looked before*, he thought.

Well, half of the mystery had been solved. Now he only needed to find out where the dog would go whenever he left the yard. "I only hope he has not been up to any mischief. I don't want anyone coming to me with an enormous bill for dog damage!" he said to himself.

It was now too late to follow Tibs, so Johnathan returned to the house. He moved around mechanically, his ears straining to detect the return of the little dog, and as if on cue, at about a quarter to one, he sensed—rather than heard—his return. Again, Tibs seemed perfectly happy with his little escapade. He had a big meal and went to sleep.

"Guess what, my little friend? I'm going to learn your game," Johnathan said.

The next time Tibs started acting up to go outside, Johnathan made sure to dress for the outdoors before letting the dog through the door. He waited impatiently for the dog to go under the fence, then followed him down the road, making sure to stay far enough behind and out of sight.

The cul-de-sac in which Johnathan lived was to the southeast of the little town. His former workplace was south of his home, the hospital was to the north, and the church Mabel used to attend was to the west. Many of her church brethren also lived in the church's direction. Since Mabel's funeral service, Johnathan had not traveled on that road, even though many of Mabel's friends had invited him to their homes and the church.

After Tibs went under the fence, he headed north, then quickly changed course and headed northwest. His pace increasing with each step he took, the little dog was soon heading west of his home. Soon, before he realized where he was, Johnathan found himself in the environs of his wife's former church. He only became aware of where he was when he heard melodious singing coming from the red brick building in front of him.

Seemingly energized by the singing, the little dog literally sprinted the rest of the way and darted through the open door of the church foyer. Johnathan was astounded. Why did the dog go into the church? Why was the foyer left open in the first place? Why hadn't someone put him out?

Suddenly, memory came flooding back. Mabel had taken Tibs to church with her. The dog had become used to going to church. It didn't do his ego much good to realize that the dog preferred the company of "those stuffy church people" to his.

"Well, at least the mystery is solved," he said gloomily. "I'd better go home."

It was a very subdued Johnathan Harry who walked the 120 chains (1.5 miles or 2.4 kilometers) back to his house. The dog had taken a very circuitous route, even though the church was not that far from his house. In thirty minutes he was home. He sat glumly, awaiting the return of his dog, who was right on time and quietly entered through the open back door. Tibs looked quizzically at his master, his head twisted to one side.

"Yes, I followed you this morning. I know you went to the church," Johnathan said gruffly, as if in answer to a question. Then he asked one of his own. "What's so interesting at that church that you are so eager to be there each Saturday?"

Of course, Tibs made no response. He just wagged his tail and waited expectantly.

Johnathan wasn't sure whether he should be amused or angry, but he was definitely disturbed. He fed the little dog, and they both took a siesta. He awoke in the late afternoon to find Tibs sitting at his feet, looking as if he was waiting for Johnathan to do something.

"Well, you've had your dinner already, and you still have snacks on your plate. Do you want to go for a walk?" Johnathan brightened at the thought of going outdoors for a while, but Tibs was not interested. "What do you want?" Johnathan asked a little impatiently.

Suddenly, his memory flashed back to the days when his late wife would busy herself around the house with Tibs at her heels. Mabel would talk to the little dog about her love for God and His love for mankind. She would sing to Tibs and read to him from the Bible. Johnathan now realized that that was what Tibs wanted.

"Me? Read the Bible to please a dog? Not on your life!" he thought "No way! No, no no!" Johnathan startled himself as he realized he was thinking aloud.

Tibs took a few steps backward, then sat and continued staring at his master. They both remained thus for a long moment. Johnathan was the first to blink.

"OK, OK, but only one psalm, and don't expect this every day." He went in search of Mabel's big family Bible—the one they had been given as a wedding present, the one in which she had carefully recorded the births and significant dates of all her children, the one in which he had noted the date of her death. Mabel had placed a number of bookmarks at some of her favorite scripture passages, and the Bible opened naturally to Psalm 23, and with the little dog sitting at his feet, for the first time in many years, Johnathan read aloud from the Bible

"The Lord is my shepherd; I shall not want ..." his voice trailed off as the old feeling of anxiety gripped him. If the Lord was his shepherd, he had not been a good sheep. He allowed the Bible to fall open naturally again, and as it did, he was looking at Psalm 119:97.

"O how I love Thy law! It is my meditation all the day," he began.

But that's not true, he thought. *The truth is, I have been a law unto myself all these years, and where has it gotten me? Sitting alone in my living room reading to my dog.*

He allowed the pages to turn again. Jeremiah 31:3 was not only bookmarked but also highlighted. He read aloud, "The Lord hath appeared of old unto me saying 'Yea, I have loved you with an everlasting love: therefore with lovingkindness have I drawn thee." Again Johnathan recoiled at the words. How could God love him? He had rejected God and denied Him and disobeyed Him too many times.

Again the Bible opened to another bookmarked passage. This was Isaiah 1:18. "Come now, let us reason together, saith the Lord," Johnathan told the little dog, even though he knew the words were for himself. "Though your sins be as scarlet, they shall be as white as snow; though they be red like crimson, they shall be as wool."

"But how can that be possible?" Johnathan asked quietly. He tried to recall all the sermons he had heard when he attended church, and all the sermonettes he had heard Mabel delivering as she worked around the house. He remembered another of her favorite passages, and this time he deliberately went to it.

"Matthew 11:28–30: 'Come unto me, all ye that labor and are heavy laden, and I will give you rest. Take My yoke upon you and learn of Me; for I am meek and lowly in heart: and ye shall find rest unto your souls. For My yoke is easy and My burden is light.'"

Johnathan was silent for a long moment after reading that passage, but Tibs didn't seem to mind. In fact, he seemed to have had his fill of Bible readings for the moment. He yawned, stretched, and went to curl up in his cot. However, Johnathan was far from satisfied. He had tacitly acknowledged that his life was incomplete, had always been incomplete, even while Mabel was alive. The problem was he had studiously rejected any effort on the part of all, including his children, to lead him to Christ. Now he felt totally alone and lost.

The following days were a blur. Johnathan mechanically went through the motions of his daily tasks. He walked and fed his dog and read to him from one of Mabel's books. Tibs was not particular. As long as Johnathan maintained a reverent manner, he listened very intently. Johnathan was even tempted to read from a secular magazine, but he knew that he needed the truth much more than the dog did, so he faithfully read from the Bible or another spiritual book.

When Sabbath morning dawned, Johnathan anticipated the dog's impatient antics, as he begged to be released outside. This time he was prepared. No sooner had Tibs darted under the hole in the fence and dashed down the road than was Johnathan hot on his trail. He knew that the little dog was aware he was following him, so on the occasions that Tibs glanced behind him, Johnathan didn't try to hide as he had done the week before.

The dog arrived at the church and, with a happy yelp, dashed toward the open foyer door. However, on this occasion, Tibs did not enter. He stood patiently at the door as his master, footsteps slowing as he neared, reached his side. Both stood at the door. Johnathan was afraid to enter, but Tibs did not want to enter without him.

Suddenly, the inner door opened, and the pastor emerged. He was beaming from ear to ear and extended both hands to Johnathan. "My dear brother Johnathan; I'm so glad you've come!" he exclaimed. He seemed not at all surprised. He paused and acknowledged Tibs, then turned his attention again to a puzzled Johnathan. "We have been praying and longing for this day," he said, "And all during this week, we've had a special fasting session each day, pleading with the Lord to open a door for you! And here you are! Bless the Lord!"

"I came because of Tibs," Johnathan said lamely. "I mean, he has been leaving the house, and I just wanted to find out ..." he began to say.

"We're just so happy that *you have* come," Nathan Brooks said, pushing open the church doors and ushering the dog and his master into the sanctuary. Without knowing why, Johnathan felt that he had come home. He looked around at all the members who smiled so warmly at him, wondering why he had always felt uncomfortable around them.

"I need to know how to get the peace that you have, that my ... that Sister Mabel had," he whispered, as he looked imploringly at the pastor.

"You have come to the right place, my brother," Nathan said. And as the church broke into the song, "There's a sweet, sweet Spirit in this place," Johnathan knew that indeed he had.

Dear Friend, our Lord will do whatever it takes to save you. Like the Father of the prodigal son, He is waiting impatiently for you to return. Like the lost sheep, you only need to call out to Him, and He will come to your aid; and like the lost coin, even if you don't know that you are lost, He will search high and low to find you. So, like the lost son, won't you return to the Father? His arms are open wide.

The Evangelist Dog

There were ninety and nine that safely lay
In the shelter of the fold
But one was out on the hills away
Far off from the gates of gold –
Away on the mountains wild and bare
Away from the tender Shepherd's care
Away from the tender Shepherd's care

"Lord, Thou hast here Thy ninety and nine
Are they not enough for Thee?"
But the Shepherd made answer,
"One of Mine has wondered away from Me
And although the road be rough and steep
I go to the desert to find My sheep.
I go to the desert to find My sheep."

But none of the ransomed ever knew
How deep were the waters crossed
Nor how dark was the night that the Lord passed through
Ere He found His sheep that was lost
Far out in the desert He heard its cry
Fainting and helpless and ready to die
Fainting and helpless and ready to die

"Lord whence are these blood drops all the way
That mark out the mountain's track?"
"They were shed for one who had gone astray
Ere the Shepherd could bring him back."
"Lord why are Thy hands so rent and torn?"
"They were pierced tonight by many a thorn."
"They were pierced tonight by many a thorn."

But all through the mountains thunder-riven
And up from the rocky steep
There arose a glad cry to the gates of heaven
"Rejoice, I have found My sheep!"
And the angels sang around the around the throne
"Rejoice, for the Lord brings back His own!"
"Rejoice, for the Lord brings back His own!"

- Elizabeth C. Clephane (1830 – 1869)

This Emptiness
The emptiness I feel is hard to describe,
This emptiness that I feel deep down inside.
Only You, O God, can fill this emptiness;
Then I'll be able to have eternal happiness.

Everywhere that You send me, I shall go,
So that the whole world will know
About a wonderful Savior like You
And worship You in everything they do.

Help me O Lord, I pray,
Never, ever to turn me from Thy way.
In serving you I'll do my best
Until the day death shall put me to rest.

— *K.V.A. St. A. Greenland*

Sabbath Night
As the sun sets on Friday evening,
Our house is filled with lusty singing—
Not songs of an unchristian nature,
But songs of praise to our Creator

At this time our thoughts are lifted heavenward,
But they're almost drowned by the noise from the road.
We read our Bible and study our quarterlies nevertheless
Because in worshipping God, we must do our best.

We retire to bed with a word of prayer,
And to see the morrow is our hope and desire.
But if we should die before we wake,
We can be sure that our soul is the Lord's to take.

For we have asked for the forgiveness of our sin
And also that we might be cleansed within.
We hope to hear our Savior say,
Well done and welcome! on that great judgment day.

—*K.V.A. St. A. Greenland*

The Mischievous Guardian Angel

Uncle Ben was well-known for the refreshing watermelons he cultivated on his farm out in the country and for the delicious mangoes that grew in his field. He was also famous for the temper tantrum he would throw whenever folks decided to help themselves to his crops without his permission.

Oh, he was a "very good Christian" and was well respected in his community. He was also very generous and gave away a substantial portion of his melons and mangoes each year. But he had one weakness. He always "lost it" when he discovered that fruits he had been saving for a particular sale or event had been raided, usually by mischievous boys from the village.

As soon as he discovered the loss, Uncle Ben would rush to the village square brandishing his very sharp machete. Then he would rant and rave and make threats for a full hour. After his anger had been vented, he would sheepishly apologize to the few villagers who had gathered to listen and ask that they forgive him. On the very next occasion he went to church, although the news of his behavior would already have reached all the members, he would relate the whole story, apologize again, and ask his church brethren to pray for him to overcome his temper tantrums.

On some occasions Uncle Ben surprised a thief in his field by chasing the culprit with his machete. Oh, deep in his heart he really didn't intend to harm anyone. He just wanted to scare them so that they would not return, and in that, he succeeded. So, eventually, only the foolish or ignorant tried to steal his crops, even if they knew he was out of the village for the day. And no one would visit his field to steal if they knew he was around.

At least that was what Uncle Ben thought. Therefore, one bright Wednesday morning as he was busy weeding a watermelon patch under a tall coconut tree, he thought his eyes were playing tricks on him when he saw a shadowy figure dart between two well-laden mango trees.

Uncle Ben, machete in hand, rushed toward the trees, but even before he got there, he knew there was no one there. *No one would be that foolish*, he thought to himself. He decided to return to his weeding, but as he turned around, another watermelon patch caught his eye, and he realized that that section needed weeding and pruning even more than the one he had been working on. He got a strong urge to move to the second patch right away, but he decided to finish with the one he had been pruning earlier.

He returned to the original patch and resumed his weeding. As he did so, a small pebble landed about three feet in front of him. *What's happening here?* he thought. *That certainly wasn't flung by my machete.* He looked around but saw no one and resumed his weeding.

Another pebble landed in front of him, this time a little closer, and this time he could distinctly hear a boyish voice say, "Hey, Ben!" The voice was definitely coming from the direction of the mango trees he had been looking at before.

"Someone is trying to play with me today," he said to himself. "I will not allow myself to become annoyed." He resumed his weeding, and although the pebbles also resumed and inched nearer and nearer, he just kept on weeding.

The next small pebble landed on the tip of Ben's nose. It stung and made him forget his resolve not to get mad.

He charged angrily toward the mango trees, machete in hand. As soon as he did so, he heard a loud creaking sound, and the entire top of the coconut tree under which he had been working came off. The fruits, boughs, and trunk trammeled into the ground, right where he had been standing only moments before. In fact, one of the nuts rolled right up against his retreating feet.

Uncle Ben shuddered as he thought what would have happened to him had he not moved. Then this question came to his mind: *Supposed I had died; would I be ready to meet my Lord?* He knew the answer to that one: Not with his temper tantrums. He looked around the field and saw no one. Of course, there was no one there. He felt that it was the Lord's doing to get him away from the collapsing tree. Ben hung his head in shame and thought, *Oh Lord what must I do? What must I do to be saved?*

Almost against his will, he found himself slowly bending his knees, bowing down, and, with his face buried in his hands, tearfully thanking God for saving his life, for by now he was convinced that the Lord had sent an angel to get him away from the impending danger. He again shuddered as he realized how stubborn he had been and how he had had almost murderous intentions toward whoever he thought had been hurling stones at him. He knew no human would have had the nerve to hurl stones at him, given the reputation he had.

"I should have known. I should have known it was You, Lord, trying to save me from myself. Please, please, Lord, I don't want to continue being angry and terrible. Please change me now!"

Ben had no idea how long he stayed on his knees pleading with the Lord, but he remained thus until he felt a calm enter his soul.

"Thank You, Lord, for hearing and for answering," he sighed, knowing finally, the peace of full forgiveness. "I will never again bring shame to Your name. I will never again be angry and sin," he vowed. He meant every word, and, with God's help, he kept every word.

> Take my life and let it be consecrated Lord to Thee
> Take my hands and let them move at the impulse of thy love
> Take my feet and let them be swift and beautiful for Thee
> Take my voice and let me sing always, only for my King
> Take my lips and let them be filled with messages from Thee
> Take my silver and my gold. Not a mite would I withhold
> Take my will and make it Thine. It shall be no longer mine
> Take my heart. It is Thine own! It shall be thy royal throne
> Take my love. My Lord, I pour at Thy feet its treasure store
> Take myself and I will be ever, only, all for Thee
> —*Frances Ridley Havergal (1836–1879)*

Judgment Time
You created me in Your likeness
So that I could worship you in the beauty of holiness.
I am a sinner, and often I stray from Thy way,
But help me, O Lord, to grow stronger each day,
So that when death's cold fingers have touched me
Or when the great clouds are rolled away,
You in Your glory I will delight to see.

I believe in You and want to serve You;
I want to worship You in everything I do.
O Lord, please help me, I pray;
And help me to serve You, come what may.

The end is near, as all the signs show.
You will claim your people then, as we all know.
I want to be among those who are chosen,
But yet I sin again and again.
So many times I have fallen short,
Yet You've forgiven my sins of every sort.

The time for forgiveness will soon run out;
There will be no forgiveness then, no doubt.

Then You will judge us accordingly,
And our reward we shall receive abundantly
So if I am one of those who are chosen,
I will live forever with you in heaven
If I am not among the chosen,
I simply will be destroyed, then.

— *K.V.A. St. A. Greenland*

Dear Friend, Christ desires that we be true representations of Him. He asks, "Why call Me Lord and do not what I say?" And Paul makes it clear that if we "have tasted of the good Word of God and the powers of the world to come" and then fall away, we crucify Christ afresh and put Him to an open shame (see Heb. 6:4–6). Let us who say we represent Christ ask the Holy Spirit to help us to be like Him. Christ admonished, "Be ye therefore perfect, even as your Father which is in heaven is perfect" (Matt. 5:48).

The Crosses

We each have a cross to bear that is uniquely our own.

Nathan was totally dissatisfied with his situation. He had just been given an assignment at work to complete a project from which two other employees had already been fired. His boss told him he had to complete the project in the time originally allotted and with the resources originally allocated, even though more than 70 percent of them had already been used up. Nathan felt sure his boss was looking for an opportunity to fire him as well.

Then his best friend, John, called to say he was dumping Nate from the upcoming fishing trip.

"My girlfriend's brother, Tom, insists on coming," John explained, adding, "I can't say no to him without annoying her, so there is no place for you. Sorry."

Shortly thereafter, Stephanie, Nathan's sister, called. She was angry and let her brother know it.

"You promised to pick up my car from the mechanic and leave it at Mom's house. Now I'm here at Mom's and there is no car. I have to meet with a very important client in Hagerstown, and I have no means of getting there!" she almost screamed.

Stephanie was a real estate agent, and those were difficult times for the real estate industry. He didn't want his sister to miss her appointment on his account, but he knew he could not leave his job to pick her up. He decided to call his girlfriend, Molly, and ask her to do him the favor of transporting his sister. She agreed but not before giving him the second degree about his carelessness and thoughtlessness.

Nathan had hardly hung up the phone before it rang again. It was his pastor, Elder James.

"How are you, Nate?" he asked cheerily. You were on my mind, so I thought I'd give you a call."

"Couldn't be worse," Nathan complained. "I feel like I have the weight of the whole world on my shoulders," he added after giving the pastor a summary of what had transpired.

Elder James chuckled. "Nate, Nate, lighten up. It's not as bad as you say. You say your job is getting to you, but think about all those persons who have no job. Then you talk about your sister and your girlfriend being annoying. Have you ever thought of all those persons who are without friends or family?"

"I'd trade places with one of them right now," Nathan said gloomily.

"Be careful about what you wish for, Nate," his pastor told him, adding, "Let me tell you a little fable. There was this young man, about your age, too, and he also thought he was carrying the weight of the whole world on his shoulders. In fact, he felt so burdened that he went to the Lord and complained that his burden was too heavy for him to bear.

"'Must I bear the cross alone and all the world go free?' the Savior asked.

"'No, Lord. I know that there's a cross for everyone, and there is a cross for me. But I truly believe that the cross I have is too heavy. Can I exchange it for another one?'

"'Certainly,' the Lord said. He took the young man to a large room. 'All the crosses are in here,' He said. 'You can leave your cross in that corner,' He pointed as He spoke, 'and choose any one you like.'

"The young man walked excitedly through the length and breadth of the room. It was much larger than he at first thought, and it was filled with crosses of every description. The young man saw long, thin crosses. He saw short, stumpy crosses. He saw huge crosses. He saw tiny crosses. He walked around the room trying on the crosses. He would rush up to a small cross and hoist it onto his shoulders, only to be stunned by its tremendous weight. He would try a thin cross, only to find that it was too long and he could not walk with it as the points kept hitting the ground. There were crosses he could not even get his arms around; they were so large.

"Who would carry a cross like that? he wondered.

"He continued walking and trying on the crosses for what seemed, to him, like hours. In fact, he was getting weary and simply could not find a cross that suited him. He was getting really frustrated. He sat for a while to collect his thoughts, thinking that he would have to go back to the Savior and say that he could not find a suitable cross. He took a last sweeping glance around the room, and as he did so, his gaze rested on what he thought was a well-proportioned cross—not too big, not too small.

"Hmm ... how come I didn't see this one before? he thought.

"He went over and tried to grip it. It fit snugly in his hands. He lifted it. It was not too heavy. He hoisted it unto his shoulder, and it felt just right.

"'Hmm … This is it! This is the one for me,' he said excitedly. 'At last, I've found the cross that is right for me.'

"With his cross on his shoulder, the young man rushed toward the door, intent on finding the Savior and thanking Him for letting him choose his own cross. The Savior was standing just outside the door, waiting.

"'Lord, Lord, thank You so much! Thank You, Lord! This is the cross I've always wanted! This is the only cross I can bear.'

"With a kind smile, the Savior said, 'My son, that was the cross you had all along. That is your very own cross.'

"So, Nate, do not be dissatisfied with your lot. Be confident that whatever you're going through is what is best for you."

Nathan was moved by the pastor's story, as he realized that he had been feeling sorry for himself and had not taken time to be thankful to the Lord for all His benefits.

"I'm really sorry, Pastor James. Please forgive me for being so ungrateful," he said.

"You do not need to ask me to forgive you," the pastor said, adding, "There is One whose forgiveness you need right now."

"You're right, elder, can you pray with me now?"

"Certainly!" the pastor said, and the two men went in prayer to the One who knows our weaknesses yet loves us with an everlasting love.

Dear Friend—especially you who are going through tremendous hardship, pain, or tragedy right now—remember the thoughts of the psalmist David:

> The Lord forgives all our iniquities
> The Lord heals all our diseases
> The Lord redeems our lives from destruction
> He crowns us with loving kindness and tender mercies
> He satisfies our mouths with good things so that our youth is renewed like the eagle's.
> The Lord executes judgment and righteousness for all who are oppressed
> The Lord is merciful and gracious, slow to anger, and plenteous in mercy
> He will not always chide; neither will He keep His anger forever

He has not dealt with us after our sins nor rewarded us according
to our iniquities
The Lord pities us as a father pities his son
He knows our frame and He remembers that we are dust
His mercy is from everlasting to everlasting upon those who fear Him
—based on Psalm 103:3–13

The Lord knows more about us than we know about ourselves, and all His thoughts about us are for our good. It is true that we cannot always see the reason for the Lord's actions, but we can rest assured that they are always for our good.

Does Jesus care when my heart is pained
Too deeply for mirth or song,
As the burdens press, and the cares distress
And the way grows weary and long?
Oh yes, He cares, I know He cares,
His heart is touched with my grief;
When the days are weary, the long nights dreary,
I know my Savior cares.

Does Jesus care when my way is dark
With a nameless dread and fear?
As the daylight fades into deep night shades,
Does He care enough to be near?
Oh yes, He cares, I know He cares,
His heart is touched with my grief;
When the days are weary, the long nights dreary,
I know my Savior cares

Does Jesus care when I've tried and failed
To resist some temptation strong;
When for my deep grief there is no relief,
Though my tears flow all the night long?
Oh yes, He cares, I know He cares,
His heart is touched with my grief;
When the days are weary, the long nights dreary,
I know my Savior cares

The Crosses

Does Jesus care when I've said goodbye
To the dearest on earth to me,
And my sad heart aches till it nearly breaks,
Is it aught to Him? Does He see?
Oh yes, He cares, I know He cares,
His heart is touched with my grief;
When the days are weary, the long nights dreary,
I know my Savior cares

—Frank E. Graeff (1860–1919), 1901

The Soursop Tree: Elder Spencer's Testimony

*In loving memory of Elder Nehemiah Spencer.
His investment pact with the Lord.*

Is anything too hard for the Lord?

Elder Nehemiah Spencer thoroughly enjoyed his walk with the Lord. During his many sermons at the New Hope Seventh-day Adventist Church, Elder Spencer was wont to say, "Since I became a Christian, the Lord has made me so good looking."

At these words, there would be the inevitable snickering, to which he would respond, "So, you all don't believe I'm good looking now? You should have seen me when I was out in the world. I was as ugly as sin."

He would go on to describe how he had been an alcoholic and would be constantly suffering from hangovers. "I always had a long face. If I looked at milk, it would curdle," he would say to subdued laughter, adding, "But thanks be to God. He not only cured me of my addiction but also cleaned up my life and gave me a beautiful wife."

Elder Spencer also often spoke disparagingly about his ability to sing, at least in this life. But he exulted in the fact he would one day be a part of the heavenly choir.

"My brothers and sisters," he would say, "even though I cannot turn a tune down here, all praise to the Almighty! When I sing His praises up there, angels will fold their wings, for they will not be able to sing the song of my redemption!"

Elder Spencer was an ardent participant in the activities of his church. He was a prominent lay activity leader and also a stalwart in building good church–community relations. One activity in which he excelled and for which the Conference recognized him several times was the church's Ingathering program at the end of each year. Elder Spencer would reach his goal faster than most people and would continue soliciting until he was one of those who had gathered the largest sums, and he would do this year after year.

Elder Spencer also did exceptionally well in the church's Investment program. No, this had nothing to do with the stock market. This was a very special effort by the church to strengthen the faith of believers and to lead them to a closer relationship with Christ. Members were encouraged to think of some aspect of their lives in which they wanted to see improvement. Some people wanted to see members of their families come to Christ. Some who were studying or pursuing careers wanted the successful achievements of their goals. Some people wanted physical, emotional, or spiritual healing.

Whatever the need was, they were to put it before Christ and ask for His miraculous intervention while endeavoring to do something sacrificial for Him as He worked on their case. Some children would faithfully put aside a part of their regular allowance. Some housewives would put aside a portion of the funds they had to run their homes. Many workers would dedicate the wages for a particular period. Some ladies would start sewing or cooking or craft projects. Those with green thumbs would plant fruits or vegetables or flowers. The proceeds from these efforts would be proudly displayed at the church's Investment service at the end of each year. Many were the astounding testimonies of the life-changing interventions of the Lord and how members had seen Him work in their lives.

One of Elder Spencer's favorite testimonies concerned his soursop tree.

The soursop, as its name suggests, is sour and soft. A member of the Annonaceae family, it is a tropical fruit with white pulp and small black seeds and with soft prickles on its green skin. This kidney-shaped fruit is not usually eaten by itself, because of its sour taste. It is often eaten with sugar (that's how the children like it), or in juices, frozen desserts, or preserves. The fruit was believed to be good for the kidney and bladder, so it was always sought after for children who were bed-wetters and for the elderly who suffered from incontinence.

Those who were fortunate enough to have a soursop tree in their yards were very popular when the fruit was in season. Most people sold the fruit at the local farmers' market or at the big market in the city. The fortunate ones were able to sell to the market vendors. These vendors would visit the yards and pick the fruit themselves. All the owner had to do was receive the money, because once a soursop tree was established, it needed no maintenance.

Elder Spencer planted his tree with high hopes. It was but a sapling then, but he looked forward to the time when all its branches and even its trunk would be laden with the tart fruit that would be in high demand; and he could earn some money from the tree.

The first few years were very hard on the tree. In its first year, a tropical storm packing winds of sixty-five miles an hour hit the area. The sapling was trammeled to the ground. In the middle of the storm, Elder Spencer ran to his tree's rescue. He raised it to a standing position and used pieces of bamboo to keep it propped up. He also tied a cord to its trunk and fastened the cord to his house. Thus fortified, the weakened tree was able to weather the storm. The next two years, the area suffered a severe drought. With its root system not yet fully established, the little tree almost died, even though Elder Spencer watered it as often as he was able.

Slowly and painstakingly, the little tree eventually grew into a beautiful luxuriant plant with wide-spreading branches. Month after month, Elder Spencer waited for the prickly green fruit to appear on the tree. He thought of the pleasure he would derive from eating the succulent tart fruit and also of how much money he would make from selling them. However, month after month, he would watch the small white flowers appear on the branches and trunk, only to see them wither and fall from the plant.

He tried everything from pruning to extra plant food and mulching. The tree only grew more luxuriant, but none of its many flowers would remain long enough to develop into fruit.

Onlookers told him that he had the male version of the tree and that it would never produce fruits, only flowers. Sadly, Elder Spencer concluded that the tree had to be hewn down. However, he decided to pray about the matter. He asked the Lord to show him whether he should cut the tree down, and he waited. He watched the tree, and he waited. He saw nothing.

It was his neighbor who startled him one morning, exclaiming, "Nehemiah, you have a large soursop on your tree."

Elder Spencer thought it was a joke, so he played along for a while.

"Yeah, man. It sure is large. I'm going to need your help to eat it," he replied.

"Well, I would be honored to have a piece of it," said his neighbor, adding, "After all, this must be a miracle fruit. Didn't we all say it was a male tree?"

Elder Spencer didn't know how to respond to that last bit, so he gave a short laugh. After that exchange he went to look at the tree again. Was this man telling the truth? If he was, how come the fruit had remained hidden from its owner's view? Hadn't he searched it with his eyes each day? Or was his neighbor just teasing? If that was the case, he did not want to appear silly.

He cautiously approached the tree, glanced furtively around, then oh-so-casually moved his gaze from the base of the tree upward. To his tremendous surprise there *was* a huge soursop among the lower branches of the tree. Not only was there one soursop; there were several soursops on the highest branches.

Elder Spencer wondered why he hadn't seen the fruits before, while he looked up at the tree, but he thanked the Lord that He had answered his prayers.

Suddenly, the idea occurred to him to dedicate the tree to the Lord.

"Lord, since I promised my neighbor a portion of one of the soursops, I'll pay for it. But I promise You, I will sell every other fruit that this tree will bear and turn over the money to You," he prayed.

And that was how it went. For years and years, Elder Spencer would turn in large sums of money for his investment project, and he never tired of telling how the Lord had turned a male soursop tree into a continuously bearing one. Many times he would make presents of some of the fruits to his friends, relatives, neighbors, and church family, but he would always make a fair assessment of all those fruits and pay for them.

The Lord blessed his efforts and proved to Him that He would be faithful in all things great and small. This was only one of the many ways in which the Lord helped to grow the faith of this Christian stalwart.

Elder Spencer is now resting, awaiting the Lord's imminent return. His story of the soursop tree is only one of the many he will relate through the ceaseless ages of eternity, of how the Lord worked marvelously in his life. Let us be encouraged by the faith and faithfulness of this saint.

Dear Friend, our Lord wants to be intimately involved in all aspects of our lives. Where our finances are concerned, He says, "Bring ye all the tithes into the storehouse, that there may be meat in Mine house, and prove Me now herewith ... if I will not open you the windows of heaven and pour you out a blessing, that there shall not be room enough to receive it. And I will rebuke the devourer for your sakes. And he shall not destroy the fruits of your ground; neither shall your vine cast her fruit before the time in the field" (Mal. 3:10, 11).

Let us be faithful and not be weary in well doing. For our Savior reminds us, "Behold, I come quickly; and My reward is with Me to give every man according as his work shall be" (Rev. 22:12). The Apostle Peter admonishes, "If ye call on the Father, who without respect of persons judgeth according to every man's work, pass the time of your sojourning here in fear" (1 Pet. 1:17).

My Prayers
Bless me O Father, please bless me
As I wait patiently at Thy feet.
Look down in love upon me dear Lord
And let me see Thy face so sweet.
Remind me, dear Lord, remind me
That I'm only a part of Thy creation.
Assure me, dear Lord, assure me
That I'm weak but Thou art strong.
Teach me, dear Lord, teach me
Teach me to go Thy way.
Train me dear Lord, train me
To never go astray.
Give me that holy frame of mind
That to all thy creatures I'll be kind;
And as my blessed Redeemer
Please save me now and forever. Amen.

— *K.V.A. St. A. Greenland*

Forgiveness: Hensler's Change of Heart

Timothy Hensler had been an alderman for the little town of Rowena for several years. He was a member of the town's development committee. He was chairman of the local school board. He was a member of the board of elders at his church, and he owned and operated the only laundry and dry cleaners not only for the town but also for several of the surrounding towns as well. There was hardly an important decision the people of Rowena made without input from Hensler. There was no major function at which he was not present. As a member of the board of elders at the Rowena First Christian Church, he was present at every service. In fact, at times he would officiate in place of the minister.

Hensler reveled in the privileged position he held. He liked to refer to himself as the "grease that keeps the wheels of Rowena turning." Naturally, the other 740 residents of Rowena loved and respected Hensler. They would tell him of their dreams and aspirations, as well as ask for his advice on any move they planned to make or any problems they were having. They would invite him to their weddings, baby christenings, birthday parties, and funerals and generally act in a way that convinced him that he was indispensable to their daily lives.

Then one day something major happened in Rowena without Hensler's input or participation. Another laundry and dry cleaner opened up at the bottom of Main Street. Hensler developed a severe case of indignation and resentment. He just could not understand his emotions. It wasn't that he feared this new business would take away his customers. His business was well established and extended well beyond the town of Rowena. It was built on excellent quality and service.

The fact was Hensler was jealous of the relationships that the new owner would develop with the members of his town. He could not bear to think of a stranger enjoying the privileges and intimacies that had been his exclusively. He was not prepared to share top billing with anyone else.

To his chagrin, his greatest fears were realized. Howard Messingar, the owner of the new store soon became a member of all the committees on which Hensler served. He soon became a member of Hensler's church, and although this fellow tried his best to reach out to Hensler, the latter stubbornly refused to have anything to do with him.

The smooth tenor of the tiny town was disturbed. Instead of commenting about the weather or who was going to get married or have a new baby, the townspeople started congregating to discuss the latest in the saga between the two men. The gist of all the discussions would be that Messingar would make another attempt to reach out to Hensler and Hensler would again rebuff him.

The situation soon became the only topic for discussion at almost every gathering. It became so grave that the minister decided that he had to do something. He invited both men to a meeting, but Hensler refused to be in the same room with someone he perceived as his enemy. The minister had to agree to meet with the men separately.

His meeting with Messingar was brief. The new store owner had nothing against his competitor and would do anything to normalize relations between them.

The minister's meeting with Hensler was a bit more challenging.

"I want to have nothing to do with this man," Hensler maintained.

"But why?" the minister asked. "He hasn't done anything to you."

"I just can't stand him. He rubs me the wrong way," Hensler insisted.

The back-and-forth went on and on. The minister reminded Hensler that he was supposed to love his neighbor as himself.

"But how can I love him when I don't like a bone in him?" Hensler asked.

"I tell you what," the minister said, "I am going to make a suggestion, and if you follow it, I guarantee that your problem with this fellow will end."

"Let me hear this suggestion," Hensler said, eagerly.

"You said you can't stand Howard Messingar. As your pastor, I am instructing you to begin praying for this man. Pray for him every day," the minister said.

"What? You can't be serious!" Hensler exclaimed.

"I couldn't be more serious," the minister said.

"I can't do that!" Hensler exclaimed. "What am I supposed to say?" he asked.

"Anything you want," the minister replied, adding, "Just make sure you include him in your prayer each day."

Hensler tried to wiggle his way out of the directive, but the minister was adamant.

Forgiveness: Hensler's Change of Heart

"If you name the name of Jesus, if you wish to remain an officer of this church, if you do not intend to spend the rest of your life full of resentment and animosity, you're strongly advised to do as I say. Those are my final words to you for now," the minister said.

The two men parted company, the minister to visit one of his homebound parishioners and the businessman to return to his place of business.

Hensler's mind was in turmoil, and he blamed Messingar for the acute discomfort he felt.

"I wish this man had never set foot in Rowena," he wailed. "I pray he would leave now!"

But the pastor's words weighed heavily on his mind. Since he was having no peace, he decided to pray about his problem.

On his knees, in the privacy of his office, Hensler said, "Lord, I do not want to pray for this man, but since the minister has insisted, I pray that you will help him to make up his mind to move from this town. Thank You, Lord. Amen."

Hensler didn't feel much better, but he was glad that he hadn't prayed for something bad to happen to Messingar. He passed the rest of the day reminiscing about how it had been in Rowena before Messingar opened up his business there.

"Yes," he mused, "things were definitely better AM [ante-Messingar], and I hope they'll be even better PM [post-Messingar]."

As was to be expected, the Lord did not answer Hensler's prayers. Messingar not only stayed in Rowena but also became even more involved in the activities of the town. Hensler resented the fact that he had to share the limelight, but he endeavored to obey the pastor's directive, and at least once per day, he would mention Messingar in his prayers. He could not bring himself to pray for bad things for someone who, in all honesty, had done him no wrong. So at first he prayed for him peripherally.

"Lord, please bless all the customers of Howard Messingar," he would say once, then, "Lord, please bless all of Howard Messingar's workers," then, "Lord, please bless Howard Messingar's friends, then, "Lord, please bless Howard Messingar's family."

When he ran out of peripheral things and people, Hensler had to start mentioning Messingar directly. With great difficulty at first, he started asking God to have mercy on Messingar. Then he started asking the Lord to bless Messingar. Soon he was doing this with less and less difficulty. As it became easier to pray for his nemesis, he found that he could tolerate Messingar a bit more.

Soon he was able to be in the same room with Messingar, even though he was still not speaking to him. After a while, to Messignar's polite greeting, he would nod curtly, but he would be taken aback by the pleasure he derived from the little exchange.

One morning, as he knelt to pray and go through the ritual of finding something good to say about Howard Messingar, Hensler had to admit that he no longer wanted the other man to leave town. For the first time since he had started the ritual, Hensler sincerely sought the Lord, not just on Messingar's behalf but on his own as well.

He ended with "Lord, please provide a way for both of us to remain in this town, if it is Your will. Amen."

Later that morning, as Messingar was leaving the post office, he was surprised to find the door being held open by Hensler. He was so surprised he forgot to give his customary greeting. The usual hustle and bustle of the little post office was suddenly stilled when Hensler called out, "Have a good day, Mr. Messingar."

You could have heard a pin drop. In fact, Messingar's jaw dropped, as did the jaws of all the staff and patrons at the post office.

Messingar sat in his car for a long while, wondering what had just happened. The postal clerk who served Hensler was barely able to concentrate. Hensler waltzed away from the post office with a song in his heart and a big smile on his face. In fact, he sailed through the day feeling lighter than he had felt in months.

In the evening, he thought he would visit with the minister and give him a progress report on his praying for Messingar. When Hensler arrived at the church office, a small group meeting was breaking up. The news of Hensler's greetings had already reached them.

"Come on in," the minister said, adding, "I believe you would want to hear what we are planning. Howard Messingar's birthday will be here in three weeks, and we're planning a surprise party for him."

Hensler waited to feel the old resentment build up inside of him, but he felt none of that old feeling.

"Great idea," he said, adding, "What do you all want me to do?"

It took a little getting used to, but the group gratefully summarized its plans for the new Hensler, and they were soon able to find him a role in the upcoming festivities. After all the activities were agreed on, they dispersed, leaving the minister and Hensler.

"You knew this would happen when you told me to pray for him, didn't you?" Hensler asked the minister.

"I didn't know it would happen. I hoped and prayed it would," the minister replied, adding, "You see, my brother, the one thing I wanted you to learn was that the most effective way to get rid of an enemy is to turn him into a friend."

Hensler laughed, saying, "I believe I was my own worst enemy, but not anymore, not anymore. I got rid of that old man, all right."

"Praise the Lord for that. Let us thank Him or all His benefits," the minister said. They both knelt, and Hensler poured out his heart in repentance and gratitude to God.

Judgment Hour

On that great resurrection day
What will you be ready to say?
That you're ready to go to heaven?
Or will you be asking for more time to be given?

So that you can be more prepared?
So that your soul can be spared?
But why didn't you use the time before?
Why did you wait until the very last hour?

— *K.V.A. St. A. Greenland*

The Law Is Key

People, church, preacher, gospel
Jesus, sin and law—just like that:
These words make no sense,
But when placed within a statement,
A full understanding is experienced.
Now listen:
The *people* go to *church* to hear
The *preacher* preach the *gospel* of *Jesus*
And how He came to die, to redeem the world from *sin*
What is sin? Sin is transgression of the *law.*
Now, my friend, remove the law from this statement,
And Jesus' sacrifice becomes redundant;
For the meaning of this whole statement,
Indeed, the meaning of a worthwhile life
Can be found in the atoning blood of Christ;
On this we know we can rely.

— *K.V.A. St. A. Greenland*

Dear Friend, remember that sin came into existence because "someone" was jealous of "another's" position. It is a natural reaction to feel resentment against others who, we feel, are stealing our thunder. But note that every time we become obsessed with "I," we will fall in the middle of "sIn." The irony is that when we harbor resentment and jealousy against another, that person will not be affected by the force of our thoughts. However, we can actually make ourselves physically ill because of the condition of our minds. Most importantly, the Bible tells us that if we regard iniquity in our hearts, the Lord will not hear us when we pray to Him. Jesus tells us in the Sermon on the Mount, "If thou bring thy gift to the altar, and there rememberest that thy brother hath ought against thee; leave there thy gift before the altar, and go thy way; first be reconciled to thy brother, and then come and offer thy gift" (Matt. 5:23, 24). We cannot say we love God, when we are harboring feelings of resentment against one of His creatures.

Our feelings of resentment are not worth it, even when we are absolutely sure that we have been wronged as a deliberate act. The Master Teacher tells us, "If ye forgive not men their trespasses, neither will your Father forgive your trespasses" (Matt. 6:15). As a matter of fact, most of what we perceive as deliberate acts aimed at hurting us are either the results of misapprehension or mistakes. We cannot read one another's minds, and we can only guess at motives. For our own peace of mind and for the sake of our own soul, let us ascribe the best motives to others, and let us treat others as we would like to be treated. "Therefore all things whatsoever ye would that men should do to you, do ye even so to them; for this is the law and the prophets" (Matt. 7:12). Paul, in writing to the Philippians, says, "Let nothing be done through strife or vainglory; but in lowliness of mind let each esteem other better than themselves" (Phil. 2:3).

Even when it is proven beyond all doubt that someone is against us, let us follow the example and instructions of Jesus. He says,

> Ye have heard it said "Thou shalt love thy neighbor and hate thine enemy." But I say unto you, love your enemies; bless them that curse you; do good to them that hate you and pray for them that despitefully use you and persecute you, that ye may be the children of your Father which is in heaven. (Matt. 5:43-45)

Peter tells us, *"Christ also suffered for us, leaving us an example that we should follow His steps, who did no sin, neither was guile found in His mouth; who, when He was reviled, reviled not again, when He suffered, threatened not, but committed Himself to Him that judgeth righteously"* (1 Pet. 2:21–23). In fact, He prayed, "Father, forgive them, for they know not what they do" (Luke 23:34).

With respect to those who deliberately hurt us, let us remember, "Dearly beloved, avenge not yourselves, but rather give place unto wrath: for it is written, Vengeance is Mine; I will repay, saith the Lord" (Rom. 12:19).

God's Plan
Do you know God's plan for you?
Do you know the things He wants you to do?
Well, God asks you to do something easy,
What some people may describe as "cheesy";
And that is to love.
Yes, this gift that was sent from above,
That's all God wants you to do:
To love Him and all others too.
But never leave yourself out,
For you're the one to spread this love about.
To me this love thing sure is right;
It's as sure as that day follows night.
And if to thine own self you're true,
Then you'll be true to all others too.

But never emphasize feelings,
For they are the strangest of things.
One minute they're going this way,
Then they're changed within the next day.

Instead, concentrate on deeds, not idle words,
For those will cut deeper than swords.
Do unto others as to yourself
And always be eager and ready to help.

So let's all spread the holy Word
To both large and small,
To the short and also to the tall,
To those we know and those of whom we've never heard.

— K.V.A. St. A. Greenland

The Cobwebs

Get rid of the spider, and the cobwebs will disappear.

Evadney Jones had been a member of the Harlem Temple Seventh-day Adventist Church for more than twenty years. She had welcomed and bidden farewell to at least five pastors. She had witnessed both the physical and spiritual birth of many a member, some of whom were still attending church and, unfortunately, some of whom were no longer walking with the Lord or fellowshipping with His people. Some had gone to sleep awaiting their Lord's return.

Evadney shook her head sadly as she contemplated the fate of a few who had gone to their graves without fully committing themselves to the Lord. She was determined that that would not be her fate. She was painfully aware that her calling and election were not yet sure, but she hoped and prayed that the good Lord would be merciful to her and enable her to, eventually, give herself fully to Him.

Toward the end of Evadney's twenty-fifth year as a member, the church welcomed yet another pastor. Evadney realized right away that there was something different about Uriah Benjamin. He seemed able to look right through her and see that she was troubled about her salvation. His sermons seemed to be aimed directly at her, and sometimes for several days after a Sabbath sermon or a Wednesday night "talk," Evadney would feel as if she was walking on clouds and was ready for translation. Within another few days, however, she would be back to her old ways and wishing that she could be a better Christian.

At prayer meetings, whenever prayer requests were solicited, Evadney always arose to thank the Lord for His goodness and mercy, but she always ended by asking her brethren to pray for her.

"Brethren, there are still some cobwebs in my life that need to be removed. Please pray for me," she would say.

Week after week, month after month, this would be Evadney's request: "Brethren, please pray for me that the Lord will remove the cobwebs from my life."

The brethren would nod expectantly as she spoke, and they could almost say the words for her as she finished. "Please pray for me that the Lord will remove the cobwebs from my life."

Things came to a head one evening. It was the final Wednesday night meeting for the year. Pastor Benjamin had been at the church for only fifteen months, but he thought he had heard Evadney's request one time too many.

Leaping from his seat as she concluded her testimony, Pastor Benjamin threw his arm in the air and said, "Hold it right there, my sister. Hold it right there. I have something to say to you. The Lord has something to say to you. You have been asking Him to clear cobwebs from your life for a long time. We have been praying that the Lord would remove cobwebs from your life for a very long time." He gestured toward the other church members, who nodded in agreement. Then he continued, "He has been removing cobwebs from your life for many, many years. But still you have a problem! Right now there are cobwebs in your life, and do you know why?"

Evadney shook her head in bewilderment. The other church members leaned forward in their seats to hear what the pastor thought was Evadney's problem. By then the pastor had regained his composure and his voice became soft, almost pleading. "My sister, there are cobwebs in your life today; there will be cobwebs in your life in the future, because you're holding on to a great big spider! Until you let go of the spider, you will not get rid of the cobwebs."

His voice was lowered so that it was barely above a whisper, but everyone heard him. In fact, you could have heard a pin drop in the church.

For what seemed like several minutes after the pastor finished speaking, there was deathly silence. Evadney stood at the front of the church like a deer caught in the glare of headlights. She felt stripped of all pretense and the veneer of righteousness she had always worn, but, strangely, she also felt liberated, and if she had even thought of being embarrassed before the other church members, she needn't have bothered, as each person, including the pastor, was examining the words he had just uttered, in light of his or her own life.

In all the years Evadney had been attending that church, she had never seen people prostrate themselves before the Lord and beg for His mercy as they did that night. In fact, she was the main petitioner. As she surrendered fully to the Lord who searches our hearts, knows our innermost thoughts, and yet loves us so, she really felt as if she was letting go of the spider that had cluttered her life for so many years—the spider of selfishness, of pride, of doubt, of procrastination, of anger, and of envy.

An overwhelming flood of love, joy, and peace engulfed her being, and she knew then and there that the Lord had not only removed all trace of the cobwebs from her life but also removed the spider as well.

Dear Friend, when the Pharisees and scribes brought to Jesus a woman who had been caught in the act of adultery, urging Him to condemn her so that they would have something to hold against Him, our Savior uttered these now famous words: "He that is without sin among you, let him first cast a stone at her" (John 8:7). And after they all retreated, He told her that He did not condemn her but that she should sin no more.

As the story goes, this woman did sin again, but Jesus did not leave her to fight her demons by herself. In the same manner, He is ready and willing to do whatever it takes to save each and every one. He now says, "I will have mercy, and not sacrifice: for I am not come to call the righteous, but sinners to repentance" (Matt. 9:13). This is not the time to play church or to reason that Jesus' return is in the future.

> Wherefore He saith, Awake thou that sleepest, and arise from the dead, and Christ shall give thee light. See then that ye walk circumspectly, not as fools, but as wise, redeeming the time, because the days are evil. Wherefore be ye not unwise, but understanding what the will of the Lord is. Be not drunk with wine, wherein is excess; but be filled with the Spirit; speaking to yourselves in psalms and hymns and spiritual songs, singing and making melody in your hearts to the Lord Jesus Christ. (Eph. 5:14–20)

"I Need the Prayers of Those I Love"
I need the prayers of those I love
While trav'ling o'er life's rugged way
That I may true and faithful be
And live for Jesus every day.

I need the prayers of those I love
To help me in each trying hour,
To bear my tempted soul to Him,
That he may keep me by His pow'r.

I want my friends to pray for me,
To hold me up on wings of faith,
That I may walk the narrow way,
Kept by my Father's glorious grace.

Refrain
I want my friends to pray for me,
To bear my tempted soul above,
And intercede with God for me;
I need the prayers of those I love.

—*James D. Vaughn (1861–1941)*

Divine Guidance
Many, many years ago, pen and paper met to form this little rhyme.
It was carefully put away and nurtured with the passing of time,
Until the day came that the little rhyme should be read,
Slowly, smoothly, so that the rhyme would play, over and over in the head,
So that hearts would be changed and lives correctly guided.

"Humble yourself, confess your sin and turn to your Savior!"
Is what the first line read for sure.
"And your God will hear and have pity on you for evermore,"
The second line read, as it sunk deep to the core.

Slowly, smoothly, as was expected, the little rhyme was read,
And it played over and over in my head.
My life was changed, and I was correctly instructed.
Now it was up to me
To allow others to be
By this little rhyme also guided.

More lines to this little rhyme should be added,
But if each reader only returns it to its safe, neatly folded,
Purposing to do what it says, but not now—another day,
It may be that many'll never find the Truth, the Life, and the Way.

—*K.V.A. St. A. Greenland*

What Grace Really Means

"Dear Lord, please give me the grace and patience I need to deal with this child," Mary Ann Benson prayed earnestly as she walked hurriedly down the corridor of her son's school. She was heading toward the principal's office—her second visit for the month—and she dreaded to hear what her son had done this time.

Sheepishly pushing open the office door after being told to enter, she nervously noted that there were four adults present, including the principal, John Stephens; and there was her son, Franklin Junior. She said her greetings, studiously avoiding the gaze of the adults, but sent an "If looks could kill" glance toward her son.

"Mrs. Benson", the principal began, "I told you earlier this month that one more incident of bad behavior on Franklin's part would warrant an immediate suspension."

Mary Ann swallowed and nodded.

The principal turned to eleven-year-old Franklin. "Son, tell your mom what you did this morning," he said quietly.

Franklin shifted his feet and looked down sullenly.

"I'm waiting," his mother said, none too patiently.

"It wasn't my fault," he began, adding, "Timmy grabbed my stuff. I told him to bring it back and he wouldn't, so I knocked him down and took my stuff."

"What stuff are you talking about?" Mary Ann asked. Her mind could handle only one detail at a time.

"He took my BB gun," the boy replied.

"Your what?! You don't have a BB gun," his mother said.

"I do, too. My dad gave it to me," Franklin said.

Mary Ann and Franklin Benson Senior had been separated for two and a half years. They had endured the usual round of couples' counseling, with no apparent chance of reconciliation. In fact, they were now discussing making their separation official. Franklin Junior spent every fourth weekend with his father, and Mary Ann had always been worried about the things his father gave into and allowed her son to do while he was with him.

"This is very serious, Mrs. Benson," the principal's voice intruded on her thoughts. "I called in the school's guidance counselor, the security officer, and the chairman of the school board. We have also contacted the office of the Superintendent of Schools, and all agree that Franklin needs a break from school. The school requires that he leave our premises now and not return until ..." he said, handing her a letter and looking at the big calendar behind his chair as he spoke, "... October 17; and on the morning of October 17, you and his father must accompany him to school, and you all must report to my office before he goes to his classes."

After more words of admonition from the principal, and apology on her part, Mary Ann was finally able to leave the office with her son in tow. Her mind was in turmoil. Frankie was really getting out of control, but to whom could she turn for support? She knew that his father would be of no help.

On the very uncomfortable ride to her mom's house, Mary Ann tried again to reach her son.

"Frankie, I'm very concerned about your behavior. Why are you constantly getting into trouble?" she asked.

This was an old discussion, and she knew all his responses.

"I don't go seeking trouble. People are always picking on me, and Dad says I'm not to let anyone walk all over me."

Mary Ann remained silent. She had always tried not to say anything negative about her estranged husband to her son. She purposed to, once again, have another "discussion" with Franklin Senior. It was not something she looked forward to.

After quickly explaining the situation to her mother, Mary Ann left the lad with his grandmother and hurried back to work. She was a legal secretary at a very prominent and busy law firm. One of her bosses was a young man, Timothy Hopkins, a brilliant and promising attorney whom she had known from high school. In fact, they had dated for a brief period and very likely would have headed for the altar, had Franklin Senior not entered the picture and swept her off her feet. She smiled wryly at that thought, because the truth was, ever since the day she met her husband, her world had been turned upside down and had still not righted itself.

Mary Ann had been one of the most popular girls in her class. Not only did all the boys want to go out with her, but she was very well liked by all the girls, too. They all knew that although she was such fun to be around, she lived by very strict principles. In fact, Mary Ann was an ardent Christian who practiced what she preached. She did not drink or smoke or use any drugs. She studied hard and got very good grades, and she treated everyone with love and respect. She was not shy to explain why she acted the way she did.

"I want everyone to see the Jesus in me," she would say.

Timothy Hopkins was also a Christian, and they attended the same church. Circumstances constantly threw them together, plus both their moms were good friends. Before long, they were a twosome. They were very comfortable in each other's company, but Mary Ann wasn't sure he was the person with whom she wanted to spend the rest of her life.

When Franklin Benson waltzed into her life, having transferred from another school during her final year in high school, Mary Ann was totally smitten. Even though her mother was very concerned and warned her about the fact that Benson was not a Christian, young Mary Ann felt sure that she could change him.

Things had not worked out that way. It was she who had changed. She stopped going to church, stopped associating with her old friends, stopped getting good grades, stopped being the upright, fun-loving person she had been.

Franklin treated her like a queen when they first met, so much so that he even won over her mother.

"He may not be a Christian, but he certainly is a gentleman. I suppose you could do worse," her mother told her.

Franklin soon became the president of the school's Young Entrepreneurs' Club and was voted the student most likely to succeed.

Against the advice of both her mother and the school's faculty, and at the insistence of Franklin, Mary Ann decided to get married right after graduation. Franklin took a job in the sales department of a large motor vehicle dealership and did very well at first. However, after a while, he started struggling to complete a sale. The couple began to have difficulty covering their expenses. Although she was a full-time student at the local community college, Mary Ann had to take on a full-time job as a receptionist at the law firm, Brighton, Bonehead, & Irons (three partners). Mary Ann had been a full time student and a part time employee at the law firm. When things got hard, she took on a full time position at the same firm, and, years later, she was still working at the firm.

Eventually, she had had to quit the community college, where she had been studying early childhood education. She decided to take online and correspondence courses and soon became a qualified paralegal.

Over the years, her husband became less and less interested in maintaining the facade of graciousness, and as he failed at his job, he took out his frustration on his wife. He never hit her, but his verbal abuse was so severe it sapped all the energy from her, and she became sullen and withdrawn at home and among her relatives and friends. She threw herself into her work and soon earned the respect and recognition of the firm's senior partners. They came to rely on her thorough research and sound opinions for many of their major cases. She became a confidante to her superiors and a role model and mentor for her coworkers.

Mary Ann and Franklin had been married for seven years when Franklin Junior was born. His birth had not been planned. Mary Ann had thought, though only fleetingly, that a child might put some life back into their marriage. She timidly broached the subject to Franklin, and his temper exploded.

"How could you think of bringing a child into our lives at this time? It's just like you to be so selfish! You only think of yourself! I am definitely not ready to be a father!"

When she got pregnant, just three months later, there was nothing Mary Ann could say to convince Franklin that she had not done it deliberately. Their relationship became even more strained, and he started spending more and more time away from home. Except for the occasional companionship of her mother, Mary Ann spent nine lonely months waiting for her husband to come home and her son to be born.

After the baby's arrival, to his credit, Franklin did try to become more caring, but the effort did not last. As soon as the congratulations and well wishes ceased, he again became the verbally abusive, resentful person he had been before. Even while she was pregnant, and particularly after the baby was born, Mary Ann fought hard against thoughts of regret about how her life had turned out generally, and particularly about bringing a child into her troubled marriage.

One good outcome of Franklin Junior's conception and birth was the fact that they brought his mother back to God. The enormous prospect of having to raise a child, most likely by herself, drove her to her knees, where she begged the Lord's forgiveness for her neglect of His will and way, and she really pleaded for His guidance and help in the upbringing of young Franklin Junior.

Mary Ann's mother had been heartbroken at the suffering her child endured. She was overjoyed when Mary Ann indicated that she wanted to renew her commitment to Christ. She knew that Mary Ann's sins were forgiven, but she still pleaded with the Lord on her daughter's behalf, as Mother knew that the consequences of her daughter's actions would still have to be borne.

The years passed quickly. As she feared, Mary Ann had to, single-handedly, be the breadwinner for herself and her son, while, at the same time, find the time to train and discipline the boy who, unfortunately, had inherited too many of his father's dominant genes. The young lad was self-centered, and resentful when he did not have his own way. Even though his mother begged him not to, he lied to and stole from her at every opportunity. His father, who by then had become only an occasional visitor to the family home, refused to help discipline the lad. In fact, on many occasions when the boy's doings were related to him, he flatly and loudly proclaimed his disbelief that the boy had done any such thing. Franklin Junior soon established camaraderie with his dad, choosing many times to misrepresent to Franklin Senior the several disagreements he had with his mother, to put her in a bad light. Soon both parents were fighting over their son more often than they fought over anything else.

The situation persisted despite Mary Ann's best efforts. At first, she asked her mother to intercede, then she appealed to various members of her church, and then she asked the pastor to counsel the family. Nothing changed. Mary Ann sought professional help. Franklin grudgingly attended the therapy sessions but stoutly refused to contribute to defraying their cost. He even more stoutly refused to adhere to any of the interventions suggested.

The decision to finally separate was inevitable. Mary Ann tried her best, for the sake of the child, to make the separation as amicable as possible, but more to spite her than anything else, Franklin Senior opted to be as difficult as he could. He moved to another town and refused to have his son for more than a single weekend each month, specifically from 6:00 p.m. on Friday to 8:00 a.m. on Monday, when the lad was supposed to be delivered to school. This arrangement posed endless problems for Mary Ann, who would too often learn, after the fact, that the father had elected to keep the boy an extra few hours or an extra day, thereby adversely affecting the Franklin Junior's attendance and punctuality record at school. In addition, after a weekend with his father, Franklin Junior's behavior, both in school and at home, would be immeasurably worse. In fact, after a while his mother started to be thankful that he saw his dad for only three days per month, because she needed all the other days to get him back to the point where his behavior was tolerable.

For more than two years, Mary Ann tried desperately to offset Franklin Senior's effect on his son, but she knew she was losing the battle. After a while she was being summoned to her son's school at least once per month. The school authorities were sympathetic and gave all the assistance they could to Mary Ann, but it was obvious to all that Franklin Junior was bent on going down the wrong path.

Mary Ann never ceased to pray that the Lord would change her son. She also asked other members of her church to pray, and, of course, her mother never ceased to pray, but they all knew that until Franklin Junior was ready, the Lord would not force him to change his ways.

At work Mary Ann tried to conceal the turmoil of her private life, but Timothy Hopkins noted the sadness in her eyes. The truth was he had resigned himself to the fact that she had chosen someone else, but he still cared about her and would have tried to help if she sought his advice. But Mary Ann was too embarrassed to tell him her concerns.

Eventually, Timothy became a partner, then senior partner at his firm. After a while, his firm moved its main office to the big city, and he went to head that section. Mary Ann deliberately neglected to keep tabs on him; she had no idea that he later became a judge.

The years passed. The divorce was finalized. Franklin Junior went on to high school, where his bad behavior followed him. Soon he was staying out late and engaging in acts that caused the police to be involved. He was busted for underage drinking and drag racing, for vandalizing someone's property, and for other criminal activities. Mary Ann was grateful that he never touched hard drugs or became a member of any street gang, but she was sufficiently bothered by what he did do. After pouring out her heart to God about her son, with the help of her pastor, she was eventually able to turn the matter over completely to the Lord. She no longer prayed for the Lord to change her son and do it now, only that He would have His will and way in both their lives.

Franklin Junior's nineteenth birthday came and went. He was still not settled on what he would do with his life. His mother would see him only occasionally, as he spent most of his time away from home. It was during one such absence that Mary Ann was awakened in the middle of the night by the shrill ring of the telephone. It was the police. They had detained her son and wanted her to come down to the police station.

"Why should I do that?" she asked, adding, "He's an adult now."

The officer explained that her son was in big trouble. He had been in a fight, and the other young man had been badly injured and was hospitalized.

"Do whatever you have to," Mary Ann said after the officer explained that her son would be kept in custody overnight.

He also explained that there was a chance the victim would not survive the night. Mary Ann tried to sound tough and resolute, but inwardly she cringed and cried for her son and for the injured young man. She prayed earnestly that the young man would not die and would recover completely.

Events moved quickly after that night. The young man recovered sufficiently for the threat of a murder charge for Franklin Junior to be averted. He was therefore granted bail. But the assault and battery charges were serious enough. In the run-up to the trial, with the prospect of a prison term hanging over his head, Franklin Junior did a lot of introspection. He started staying home more often, and his mother, for the first time in years, got a chance to really talk to him. She reminded him of the many long walks and tender talks they had had when he was little; of how he had eagerly given his heart to the Lord when he was only five years old.

"What happened, son?" she asked, shaking her head sadly.

"I've done a lot of dumb things, Mom," Franklin Junior acknowledged. He begged her to forgive him for the way he had hurt her, and thanked her for standing by him over the years, and especially in the trouble he was in. He also told her how hurt he had been when his parents separated.

"For a long time I blamed you," he told Mary Ann, adding, "Since Dad was the fun-loving one and he allowed me to do whatever I wanted, I thought he must be the better parent, and I so badly wanted to be with him all the time. Even when he moved away, I believed you had something to do with his not being able to live here anymore and that it was you who didn't want me to go to live with him."

Mary Ann cringed as her son spoke, but she kept silent, sensing that by now she did not need to defend herself.

Franklin Junior continued, "Many of the times when I left home and you thought I was with my friends, I would hitchhike over to Dad's house. Most of the times he wouldn't be home, but I would just hang around until he returned. Even though he didn't appear pleased to see me, when he did come home, I still did not get the message that he didn't want anything to do with me."

"How did you find that out?" Mary Ann's voice was barely above a whisper.

Franklin took a deep breath. He smiled wryly. "Honestly, I guess I've always known. I just wouldn't admit it. But things came to a head one night, when I was about fifteen. I had wanted to go with some friends to a rock concert in Atlanta. You told me I couldn't go, and I was furious. I couldn't wait to thumb a ride. I used all my spending money to hire a cab to take me to Dad's house. I planned to beg him once again, to allow me to go and live with him."

He paused and again took a deep breath. "Dad was home that night, but he was not alone." He paused and glanced at his mother, but she was staring into the distance with a pained expression on her face.

"Well," he continued, "it wasn't pretty. He told me that he had never wanted children; never wanted me; that it would have been better if you had aborted me."

At this, Mary Ann cried out as she imagined the pain her child had suffered. She reached up and pulled his head down to her bosom and rocked him gently as he spoke.

"For a while, I was inconsolable. I already felt that you had been against me and then when I heard those things from Dad, I felt like an orphan, but the tragedy was— both my parents were still alive."

"I'm really, really sorry, son," Mary Ann began. "I suppose I could have spared you some of that pain by explaining the type of person your father was from the very beginning, but I did not want to influence you unduly. Plus, I really hoped and prayed, and I actually asked, that he would put aside our differences when he had to deal with you. Like you, I suspected but would not admit that he had a bad influence on you. I guess I was thinking that a bad dad was better than no dad at all."

"Don't blame yourself, Mom," Franklin Junior said. That's been several years ago, and I've known for a long time about the great sacrifices you've made for me. Several times I would sneak into the house and hear you praying for me. It would make me feel guilty, but I was also filled with a lot of anger, and that caused me to do even more crazy things. Soon I was caught in a vicious trap from which I couldn't escape. It took a near disaster to break the spell."

For the first time, he explained to his mother what had transpired that fateful night when he almost committed murder. He explained that he and some friends had been bar hopping, getting more and more drunk as the evening wore on. At last, they went to a club in a very crime-ridden section of the city. If he hadn't been so drunk, he probably would not have gone there, but by then he was not thinking straight. When another patron started bad-mouthing him, he flew into a rage and attacked the young man.

"The strange thing," he told his mom, "was that even though my friends were telling me to calm down, I kept hearing this voice saying 'Kill or be killed! Kill or be killed!' I now know it was the devil and he was really out to destroy me that night. But do you know what? Jesus was also there; and at one point, when I stabbed at the young man with my knife, I definitely felt someone pull back on my arm, and that is the reason he was not stabbed fatally. The doctors said if the knife had gone just a fraction of an inch deeper, it would have entered his heart."

"Thank God things turned out that way," Mary Ann said. She went on to explain that for some time before she had been praying that the Lord would have His way in her son's life.

"You noticed that I stopped nagging you. I stopped criticizing you. I stopped begging you to change your ways. I simply turned everything over to God and asked Him to have His own way with you," she said.

"Well, He answered your prayers," Franklin Junior said. "He had His way that night, and He has been having His way with me ever since. I now know and acknowledge how much God loves me and how terrible I have been. I've asked Him to forgive me. In fact, I've asked just about everyone I've wronged to forgive me, and it was a very long list," he said with a smile.

"I am so happy for you, my son," Mary Ann said, adding, "From now on we can both have the confidence that if you allow the Lord to lead you, you will make the right decisions."

Franklin Junior smiled, then became serious. "I've asked the Lord to forgive me for hurting this young man, and He has forgiven me, but I still will have to deal with the consequences of my actions. Mom, I do not want to go to prison. What shall I do?"

"You might not get a prison sentence. You could be fined," she said. But then it was her turn to frown. "But the fact is, son, we do not have any money, and I don't know where to get any money at this time."

They both sat in silent contemplation for a while; then the mother spoke. "I tell you what, let us place this matter firmly in God's hands. Let us trust Him to deal with this matter, as it is definitely too hard for us."

Mother and son prayed together and then prayed individually, and both decided to trust the Lord to bring about the outcome He desired.

The day of the trial dawned, and Mary Ann and Franklin, after again petitioning the Lord, went to hear the adjudication of the matter.

After finding the room in which the trial would take place, Mary Ann and Franklin took their seat in the back and remained lost in their own thoughts until Franklin Junior's name was called. He rose and announced his presence and was summoned before the judge. His mother accompanied him to the front of the courtroom.

Franklin Junior hung his head in shame as the charges were read out. He was then asked what his plea was.

"Guilty as charged," he said.

"Is there anything you would like to say before I pass sentence on you?" the judge asked.

Franklin Junior hung his head and said, "No, Your Honor."

But there was something about the judge's voice that made Mary Ann look at his face intently. It looked like … but it could be … could it be… "Judge Hopkins?"

"Yes, Madam?"

She had said the words more to confirm her suspicion than for any other reason, but when Timothy Hopkins turned his full attention to her, she had to say something.

"Your Honor, my name is Mary Ann Benson. I am the mother of the accused. May I approach the bench?"

The judge looked from mother to son, then said sternly, "You can say what you have to say in open court."

Mary Ann began an impassioned plea for her son, stating that it was true that the young man had lost his way and done so many wrong things, but that he had made an about-face and now only wanted to serve the Lord. She begged the court to give him a chance to live right from then on.

With an impatient expression on his face, Timothy Hopkins waited until she was finished, then he used the information she had just shared to show every reason why Franklin should be made to pay dearly for his crimes. He concluded, "For what you have done, you deserve to be locked away for a long time, but I do not think justice would be served by having you repose in some facility at the tax payers' expense. However, can you give me a good reason why I should not impose a hefty fine on you?"

Again Mary Ann tried to get his attention. She raised her hand.

"What do you wish, Mother?" Hopkins asked.

"Permission to approach the bench, please Your Honor, she pleaded.

He motioned her up with his hand.

"With tears in her voice she whispered, "Your Honor, Timothy, I am very sorry that things have turned out this way, but I assure you that my son has learned his lesson. He has changed, so I beg you, do not send him to prison."

"I said I am going to fine him!" the judge said sternly.

"But that's the problem," she whispered, "We ... We have no money ..." Her voice trailed off, and her eyes pleaded with him.

For a brief moment, Timothy felt overwhelmed by her grief. Then he snapped, "Go back to your place. This conversation is over!"

Mary Ann walked back over to her son and took his hand in hers, waiting for the ominous words.

Judge Hopkins spoke for a few more minutes about the folly of youth and other things. Mary Ann could not concentrate. Finally, she heard her son gasp and realized that the judge had passed his sentence. The fine was the highest that the charges allowed.

"What do we do now?" she asked.

"Report to the clerk of the courts," the judge told her, motioning to a door to the right of the room.

She entered the room with her son, and they waited for what seemed like hours. Finally, a kind-looking middle-aged man entered the room.

"Mrs. Benson and young Benson, you are now free to go," he said cheerily.

"But what about the fine?" she said, "We can't pay it. We have no money."

The gentleman smiled at her, "Let not your heart be troubled," he said. "All has been paid."

"What do you mean?" they both asked.

"The fine has been paid," the man repeated.

"But how?" May Ann asked

The clerk of the court opened his ledger and showed them a personal check made out to the court in the exact amount of the fine, by Timothy Hopkins.

Mary Ann could not hold back the tears that had been threatening to flow all day. Her son comforted her, and the man disappeared.

They stayed until the end of the day so that they could talk to Timothy Hopkins.

"I cannot thank you enough," Mary Ann began.

"You don't have to," he cut her off, then looked directly at Franklin Junior. "Regard it as the down payment on the new life your mother spoke about. Never must you set foot in a courtroom again, unless it is to be a witness, a juror, a lawyer, or a judge," he said with a smile in his voice.

After chatting with him for a few minutes more, Mary Ann and Franklin Junior headed home, relieved and grateful that God had worked things out.

"Now I fully understand what grace means," he said. "I have been given the chance to live in this world as a free man at Judge Hopkins' expense, and I have been given the chance to live in eternity at Christ's expense.

"Amen! Thank You, Lord!" said Mary Ann.

What is Love ... Really?
If God sent Jesus to die for us,
The only Son of His,
Then is not that a true illustration
Of what real love is?
Jehovah, our Lord and God
Whom by angels is worshipped
Would prefer
For us lowly beings to call Him Father.
Yet how do we treat Him after, for us,
He demonstrated such love?
We, pitiful wretches, barely find time
To whisper to Him a very brief prayer.

—K.V.A. St. A. Greenland

Touched by an Angel:
Eulene's Testimony

It was a special Sabbath at the New Hope Seventh-day Adventist Church. An evangelistic series would be starting in a few weeks, and the membership had been asked to fast and pray for the outpouring of the Holy Spirit and for the Lord's blessing on the upcoming events.

A large percentage of the brethren had decided to fast from sunset Sabbath eve on Friday to the close of the Sabbath on Saturday. Things were going well. As usual, the day started with devotional reading at 9:00 a.m. This was followed by a rousing song service at 9:15. The Sabbath school superintendent and the other leaders marched onto the platform promptly at 9:30, and the morning's activities proceeded apace.

During the divine service, the announcement was made that those who were fasting could remain behind for another service if they wanted to. The first elder, Christopher Thorpe, would lead out.

At the conclusion of the divine service and after several minutes of greetings and fellowship, most of the members went home for lunch. Those who were fasting, plus a handful of supporters, a total of about fifty people, assembled in the small sanctuary. The session started the usual way: with the soulful singing of some spiritual songs, reading from the Scriptures, and one or two testimonies. It was then time for our first session of prayer.

Elder Thorpe asked for prayers from each side of the aisle and said he would pray at the end. We all knelt, and the prayers began. Some were fairly long. A few were brief, but all were sincere, as members poured out their hearts before the throne of God. Finally, it was Elder Thorpe's turn, and he prayed a simple, brief prayer, no doubt with his mind on the rest of the program.

It was at this point that the meeting was taken completely out of the hands of Elder Thorpe and out of the hand of each person present. After he finished praying, Elder Thorpe said amen. And the members all said amen.

The natural expectation, after this, was for all to rise from their knees, but for several seconds after the amens, nobody moved.

The seconds ticked by. Still nobody moved.

Elder Thorpe said, "Let us rise up now, brethren." Still nobody moved.

At that moment, I half-opened one eye and peered around. Everyone was still kneeling, including Elder Thorpe, who had told us to rise.

He said it again. "Let us rise, brethren."

I decided to obey him and started to rise. At that point I felt a gentle but firm pressure on my left shoulder, and as hard as I tried, I could not move.

Suddenly, from the other side of the aisle, across from me, I heard a voice speaking. Again I half-opened my eyes to see who was speaking. The voice was coming from a good friend of mine, Sister Marjorie Moncrieffe, but it was not her voice I was hearing.

She said, "Elder Thorpe, do not tell the brethren to rise. They need to remain on their knees. There is a lot more to be said. The church needs to have meetings like this more often."

The air was electrified. I sensed that we were in the presence of something awesome, but I had no word or thought to describe what was happening. Since no one was getting up and since the sister had spoken so authoritatively, Elder Thorpe said, "OK, brethren, we'll go into another season of prayer."

Well, he needn't have said "another," because it was as if the meeting had just begun; as if the praying had just begun. There was weeping. There was lamentation. There were shouts of exultation and joy as we, totally liberated from all inhibition, bared our souls before God and before one another.

I couldn't speak to what other members were experiencing, but at a particular juncture, all eyes still closed, all heads bowed, with the sound of several members weeping or rejoicing all around me, I heard what I can only describe as "a still, small voice" speaking over my left shoulder and into my left ear.

It distinctly said, "Greenie, do you want to know what your problem is?"

Now, there was only one person who called me "Greenie." It was a dear old friend whose advice I had often sought and followed. But she was not at the meeting, because she was not well at the time. However, hearing that name instantly made me attentive and put me at ease.

I nodded in my heart, and the voice continued.

"You have two problems: self and appetite," it said.

I have no idea who was speaking to me, but I am positive that what was being said was true.

Only after everyone had received a chance to speak, were we finally allowed to rise. It was as if bands that were binding us were finally loosed. The meeting then proceeded as usual, culminating just before the regular afternoon program. We remained for all the programs and only left long after sunset, when all the services were complete.

The strange part was, no one commented on what had transpired earlier. I remember walking home that evening on very wobbly legs. Even my voice sounded very strange, very subdued, to me.

It was several weeks later, after the evangelistic series had ended, that we were having another fasting service and a young man, a visitor from another church, got up and testified.

"I am so glad I was here to experience the outpouring of the Holy Spirit," he began.

Everyone looked at him expectantly.

"Yes, brethren," he continued, "I only decided on a whim to visit New Hope that Sabbath, and I also decided, on a whim, to remain for the fasting service, since I had not been fasting. But what an experience! I bless the Lord for it and wouldn't have missed it for anything."

He went on the describe how he had tried to rise from his knees and found that he could not, how he had heard the instructions from God coming through the sister, how he had been broken by the presence of the Holy Ghost.

Only after this brother's testimony did the members of New Hope get the courage to relate their own experiences, and it was remarkable how similar they all were.

Sister Moncrieffe testified that she had no idea what had come over her, but she had just been compelled by an overwhelming need to urge the church to remain on its knees. All said that they had felt the same restraint that I had felt when I had tried to rise, and all had experienced a wonderful release and sense of communion. To this day, that incident remains one of the high points of my Christian life.

Dear Friend, that day I had a foretaste of the Master's presence—and what an awesome experience it was. I know that the voice that spoke to me told the truth. My greatest problem at the time revolved around self and appetite. The unfortunate thing is that I believe that those two vices are still my greatest challenges. However, my selfishness had more to do with doubt about what I can do, rather than with thinking that I was the star of the show, but I was nevertheless consumed with selfishness.

In the intervening years, God has shown His awesomeness so magnificently to me and has let me know that His grace is sufficient for me, that His strength is made perfect in my weakness (see 2 Cor. 12:9). I now know fully that without Him I can do nothing but that I can do all things through Christ, who strengthens me. With this knowledge, I can only say, "What a mighty God we serve!" I have learned to lean on Jesus and to depend on Him totally and to draw on His power to accomplish His will. And I'm learning more and more each day to die to self and to let Jesus control all aspects of my life, including my appetite. Praise His name!

> For I know the thoughts that I think toward you, saith the LORD, thoughts of peace, and not of evil, to give you an expected end. Then shall ye call upon Me, and ye shall go and pray unto Me, and I will hearken unto you. And ye shall seek Me, and find Me, when ye shall search for Me with all your heart. (Jer. 29:11–13)

I long for the day when I will completely lose myself in Him and will be able to confidently say:

Not I, but Christ, be honored, loved, exalted;
Not I, but Christ, be seen, be known, be heard;
Not I, but Christ, in every look and action;
Not I, but Christ, in every thought and word.

...

Not I, but Christ, my every need supplying;
Not I, but Christ, my health and strength to be.
Christ, only Christ, for body, soul, and spirit;
Christ, only Christ, here and eternally.

...

—*Ada A. Whiddington, 1891; arranged by Fannie F. Bolton, 1900*

"Revelation 14:6–12"
There was an angel who had the gospel,
And his duty was to preach the message to the people.

And he said:
Give honor and glory to God,
For the hour of His judgment has come;
So you should worship Him
Who has made this earth and also His entire kingdom.
And there was a second angel saying,
Babylon is fallen, yes, that great nation
That made all civilizations
Drink of her cup of fornication.
And yet a third angel followed
And, with a loud voice, he said
That anyone worshipping the beast and his image
And receiving its mark, whether on hand or head,
The same shall drink of God's indignation
In front of the sacred Lamb and His holy angels;
They shall be cast into eternal damnation
With no rest, because of their condemnation.

—*K.V.A. St. A. Greenland*

Sunday Law
For years about the Sunday law we heard,
But it seemed some didn't believe one word,
Until it came one day in a radio broadcast,
Ellen G. White's prediction was coming to pass.

For some the broadcast was a stern warning
That they should be ready for the Lord's returning;
But for others, in fact, the vast majority,
It was just another news item
Soon to be relegated to history.

"Fear God and keep His commandments!"
In this statement lies the whole duty of man,
But the way things are today, it seems
This is the one thing mankind doesn't understand.

"How are things today?" the question might be asked.
If you look at our list of priorities, you'll see God last.
In days of old God was not only first,
But indeed He was the center of the human race.

Today we pitiful beings do not even recognize
That our souls are athirst.
The vast majority of us continue on
At a steady pace, to eternal destruction.

—*K.V.A. St. A. Greenland*

Yes, Dear Friends, of this we are sure: Christ said He has gone to prepare a place for His friends and brethren. He says His friends are those who love Him, and those who love Him keep His commandments (see John 15:10, 14). He said, "If a man love Me, he will keep My words: and My Father will love him, and We will come and make Our abode with him" (John 14:23). The Creator of the universe not only called us "friends" (John 15:15) but also said, "Whosoever shall do the will of My Father which is in heaven, the same is My brother, and My sister, and My mother" (Matt. 12:50). What a wonderful privilege has been afforded us! Therefore, Paul reminds us,

> Owe no man any thing, but to love one another: for he that loveth another hath fulfilled the law. ...Love worketh no ill to his neighbor: therefore love is the fulfilling of the law. And that, knowing the time, that now it is high time to awake out of sleep: for now is our salvation nearer than when we [first] believed. (Rom. 13:8,10, 11)

Let us remember that He who cannot lie will keep His promise to return one day and will take with Him His reward, to give to each one of us as our work has been. We will either hear, "Well done, good and faithful servant. ... Enter thou into the joy of thy Lord" (Matt. 25:23) or we will be cast into outer darkness because of our unfaithfulness.

We have to realize that "the night is far spent, the day is at hand" and we must "cast off the works of darkness" and "put on the armor of light." We must shun riotous living, drunkenness, promiscuity, blatant disregard for others, strife, and covetousness. Let us put on Christ, instead, and "walk honestly, as in the day" (see Rom. 13:12–14). Let us lay aside every weight and the sin [breaking of God's law] that so easily besets us, and let us run with patience the race that is set before us (see Heb. 12:11). Christ promises the following:

> He that overcometh shall not be hurt of the second death. To him that overcometh I will give to eat of the tree of life which is in the

midst of the paradise of God. To him that overcometh will I give to eat of the hidden manna, and will give him a white stone, and in the stone, a new name written which no man knoweth saving him that receiveth it. And he that overcometh and keepeth My works unto the end, to him will I give power over the nations; And he shall rule them with a rod of iron. As the vessels of a potter shall they be broken to shivers: even as I received of My Father. And I will give him the morning star. He that overcometh, the same shall be clothed in white raiment; and I will not blot his name out of the book of life, but I will confess his name before My Father, and before His angels. To him that overcometh will I make a pillar in the temple of My God, and he shall go no more out: and I will write upon him the name of My God, and the name of the city of My God: and I will write upon him My new name. To him that overcometh will I grant to sit with Me in My throne, even as I also overcame, and am set down with My Father in His throne. (Rev. 2–3)

May the Lord keep us faithful until He comes.

TEACH Services, Inc.
PUBLISHING

We invite you to view the complete
selection of titles we publish at:
www.TEACHServices.com

We encourage you to write us
with your thoughts about this,
or any other book we publish at:
info@TEACHServices.com

TEACH Services' titles may be purchased in
bulk quantities for educational, fund-raising,
business, or promotional use.
bulksales@TEACHServices.com

Finally, if you are interested in seeing
your own book in print, please contact us at:
publishing@TEACHServices.com
We are happy to review your manuscript at no charge.

www.ingramcontent.com/pod-product-compliance
Lightning Source LLC
Chambersburg PA
CBHW070543170426
43200CB00011B/2532